Facing Forever

Planning for Change in Family Foundations

Elaine Gast

COUNCIL *on* FOUNDATIONS

MISSION

The Council on Foundations is a membership organization that serves the public good by promoting and enhancing responsible and effective philanthropy.

VISION

In an environment of unprecedented change and potential, the Council on Foundations in the twenty-first century supports philanthropy worldwide by serving as

- *A trusted leader.* Promoting the highest values, principles and practices to ensure accountability and effectiveness in philanthropy.
- *An effective advocate.* Communicating and promoting the interests, value and contributions of philanthropy.
- *A valued resource.* Supporting learning, open dialogue and information exchange about and for philanthropy.
- *A respectful partner.* Collaborating within a network of philanthropic and other organizations working to promote responsible and effective philanthropy.

STATEMENT OF INCLUSIVENESS

The Council on Foundations was formed to promote responsible and effective philanthropy. The mission requires a commitment to inclusiveness as a fundamental operating principle and calls for an active and ongoing process that affirms human diversity in its many forms, encompassing but not limited to ethnicity, race, gender, sexual orientation, economic circumstance, disability and philosophy. We seek diversity in order to ensure that a range of perspectives, opinions and experiences are recognized and acted upon in achieving the Council's mission. The Council also asks members to make a similar commitment to inclusiveness in order to better enhance their abilities to contribute to the common good of our changing society.

COUNCIL *on* FOUNDATIONS

1828 L Street, NW, Suite 300
Washington, DC 20036-5168
202/466-6512
www.cof.org

Table of Contents

Part Two—SOLUTIONS

Facing Forever: *Planning for Change in Family Foundations*

Part Three—SAMPLES

CONCLUSION

SUPPLEMENTARY SOURCES

Acknowledgments

To the Council on Foundations' Committee on Family Foundations, for giving voice to the needs of family foundation board members and staff.

To the editorial advisory group, whose vision and foundation experience shaped this volume.

Diana Gurieva
Executive Director
Dyson Foundation

Katharine Mountcastle
Trustee
The Mary Reynolds Babcock Foundation

Diane Bernstein
Vice President
Diane & Norman Bernstein Foundation

Nathanael W. Berry
Program Director
The Sandy River Charitable Foundation

Conrad Hilton
Trustee
Conrad N. Hilton Foundation

Preface

As family foundations mature, their options and opportunities become more complex.

Message from Family Foundation Services

Most of the family foundations in existence were formed in the last 20 years. Yet at the Council on Foundations, a 54-year-old membership association, we are fortunate to work with many that were established earlier—foundations with third-, fourth- and fifth-generation family members. It's through our work with these long-established foundations that we're better able to "predict the future" for our many newer members and help them prepare for it.

One prediction is this: As family foundations mature, family members frequently become more diverse—in where they live, in their beliefs and in their grantmaking style. These differences confront the families with many choices and questions. Can the foundation continue as an effective and rewarding entity? What are the practices and models that will allow it to do so? Would it be better to terminate the foundation, split it into pieces or place its assets elsewhere?

Facing Forever: Planning for Change in Family Philanthropy will help families begin to answer these questions and guide foundations as their options and opportunities become more complex.

Karen Green
Managing Director
Family Foundation Services
Council on Foundations

Introduction

As family foundations mature, how can they manage, much less plan for, the challenges of change?

Each successive generation in family foundations faces its own unique challenges. However, as the foundation grows in age and size, so do the challenges in their frequency and complexity. Often, the first major challenge a foundation encounters is a shift in leadership—the original donor may die, for example, or become too aged or ill to lead the foundation. The family may become too large for all to participate on the board, or too small to produce a succeeding generation of board members. Perhaps the family becomes geographically dispersed, or uninterested in the original intent the donor prescribed for the foundation. Differences and disagreements may affect both personal relationships and foundation performance.

Family foundations may confront a number of challenges beyond a shift in leadership: divorce, death and discord among the family, to name a few. These are the hardest and most intimate issues to talk about. Yet, talking about them *before* the family is under stress can help the foundation board develop a game plan for how to respond.

Are there ways to prepare for these challenges in advance, to circumvent or resolve them? Because of the individual nature of family foundations, there may not be a one-size-fits-all solution to every situation. But there *are* steps every family foundation can take to prepare for the transitions ahead and to cope with challenges in the present. This book will show you these steps.

Simple preventive strategies can circumvent problems within family foundations before they start and help foundations find opportunity in times of change.

JIMMY, SIXTH-GENERATION PAIN IN THE ASS

How to Use This Book

Family foundations can find opportunities even in times of great change and crisis. This book will help resolve problems your foundation faces now or will likely face in the future. It will arm you with the tools, stories and resources to help you prepare for current and future transitions. At the very least, it will help get your board talking. By raising difficult issues, this book will make it easier for your board to discuss and plan for highly personal, highly probable possibilities.

There are three major sections in this book: *Scenarios, Solutions* and *Samples.*

Part One, *Scenarios*, deals with specific challenges that mature family foundations face, illuminating the many forms change might take in your own foundation. In Part One, you will find three chapters. The first presents issues of *Family Involvement*—board recruitment and selection, succession, and geographic dispersion. The second chapter, *Dealing with Differences*, discusses personal tensions and confrontations—for example, divorce, disagreements, and typical board conflicts. Chapter three, *The Unexplained and Inevitable*, presents hard human issues—primarily, the death of a foundation leader and all the changes that can ensue. This chapter addresses how the family can cope with death, how the foundation can manage a rapid change in leadership, and what happens if the foundation experiences a change in assets—often as a result of a large bequest from the deceased. By raising these issues in a frank, honest way, Part One reminds family foundations how they can use challenges as a catalyst for positive change.

Simple preventive strategies can circumvent problems within family foundations before they start and help foundations find opportunity in times of change.

Part Two, *Solutions*, describes alternative futures for foundations undergoing challenge and looking to make a change. The first section, *Grantmaking Alternatives*, discusses the advantages and limitations of changing the mission and discretionary grantmaking. The second section, *Structural Alternatives*, outlines the many choices a foundation has if and when it decides to split, spend down, merge or terminate.

Part Three, *Samples*, offers sample documents that your board may find. helpful to use or amend. Most of these samples come from your colleagues who have generously shared what works best for them. Use this section as a menu of tools from which you may pick and choose as you need.

The book includes lists of *Supplementary Sources* to keep you apprised of the many opportunities available to you in the philanthropic field. Whatever your role in the foundation—board or staff, veteran member or new—you will learn strategies, successful techniques and advice from your colleagues on managing the many changes that arise when foundations mature.

In Their Own Words:

No Challenges in Your Family Foundation? Just Wait!

"When I joined the Rasmuson Foundation, my work was limited to reviewing grant applications for the board. Family foundations 'issues' like succession, geographic dispersion, donor intent didn't concern the board or me. Guess what? They're ALL issues now. Amazing how quickly that happens. They are universal issues for family foundations. As a staff, the most challenging part of the job is to be in the role where you are not dominating, but facilitating the ability of the family to carry out their philanthropic goals."

—*Diane Kaplan, Rasmuson Foundation*

A Word of Caution:

Self-Dealing and Disqualified Persons

As a board member or staff of a family foundation, you must be aware of the legal rules governing family foundations. While this book is not intended to be a legal reference, some of the activities discussed herein could have legal ramifications if not followed appropriately. Proper procedures and board member education can minimize the risk to you and your foundation.

A private foundation is generally prohibited from self-dealing—entering into any financial transaction with "disqualified persons" (as the language of the law calls them). Disqualified persons include certain public officials, foundation managers, family members of disqualified persons, substantial contributors, and corporations and partnerships in which disqualified persons hold significant interests.

One of the few exceptions to this rule is paying reasonable compensation to a disqualified person for personal services that are necessary to fulfilling the foundation's charitable purposes. Violations will result in an initial penalty tax equal to 5 percent of the amount involved, payable by the self-dealer.

All of these rules and regulations can be found in *Family Foundations and the Law: What You Need to Know*, by John Edie, Council on Foundations, www.cof.org. For guidance on any legal issues, a qualified attorney should always be consulted.

Part 1

Scenarios

COUNCIL *on* FOUNDATIONS

*"Before we begin this family meeting, how about we go around
and say our names and a little something about ourselves."*

Chapter 1: Family Involvement

In this chapter:

- Board Recruitment and Selection
- Succession
- Geographic Dispersion

As a family foundation matures, family involvement can become an increasingly pressing issue. In its first and second generation, the board might not include more than the donor couple and their children. By the third generation and beyond, however, a crop of grandchildren, great-grandchildren and cousins may wish to be included. The family may be large, with too many members jockeying to get onto an already unwieldy board. Or the family might have dwindled in size, leaving few able or willing to take on the responsibility of running the foundation. What's a board to do when there is no one to take over? Should it close its doors, open board membership to the community, or perhaps transition from a family to an independent foundation? Regardless of whether a family is large or small, a board will grapple with bringing on new members.

As a board first considers new board members, it must determine a definition of *family member* for the purpose of board service. Current members will create a policy for who is eligible to serve on the board and what the criteria for membership will be. By creating

"Regardless of whether a family is large or small, a board will grapple with bringing on new members."

—Karen Green,
Managing Director,
Family Foundation
Services,
Council on Foundations

such a policy early, the board can ease the transition later when it is time to engage successive generations. The goal is to help build foundation interest and engage and eventually recruit younger members of the family to the foundation.

For some foundations, location is an issue. Many foundations face the dilemma of geographic dispersion, with family members who live all over the country, sometimes even the world. At its simplest, it becomes a practical challenge to hold board meetings; at its most difficult, it's a philosophical challenge to keep board members interested in the foundation at all.

Read this chapter to learn more about the above challenges, and how your colleagues have worked through them.

Board Recruitment and Selection

Who Serves on the Board?

In any family, it may be hard to choose who serves on the board. Because families often grow exponentially, the family foundation must review and renew its organizational structure to ensure long-term operations. Some foundations organize family participation by providing the opportunity to any and all who are interested. Others base involvement on capabilities, personalities or expertise of family members, and/or by democratically voting for members they think will work well in fulfilling board responsibilities. Still other families use a nominating process, which is then voted on by the board or by all family members.

The first question boards will face is this: Who in the family is eligible for board service? Some boards:

- Include the immediate family only, while other boards include extended family members such as aunts, uncles, cousins, etc.

- Allow only lineal descendants. Others allow spouses a place at the table and consider what will happen in the event of divorce.

- Automatically award children a place on the board, while other boards ask children to *earn* their place by showing interest, attending meetings and conferences and meeting other requirements as set by the board.

When families have a number of different branches, each branch, or nuclear family, may select a designated number of representatives to the board. Each branch representative might serve for a term and then trade off with a sibling or parent to give everyone a chance to participate. Similarly, when families have more than one generation of adults, boards can elect to have each generation represented, or fill a designated number of seats from among different generations.

However the family foundation board is structured, board members should involve as many family members as is practical—and no more—while ensuring that each person finds fulfillment from his or her involvement.

Family involvement is not the only consideration for who serves on the board. In addition, boards must think about the following questions:

- Should nonfamily members from the community serve on the board? If not, how will the board incorporate the community's perspective or the person's subject-area expertise?

- Should there be minimum and maximum ages for board service?

- What are the responsibilities of each board member? How will board members be removed if they fail to meet their responsibilities?

- Should there be term limits or rotation—for example, a maximum of two six-year terms or on for two three-year terms, off for one term?

With so many factors to consider, it helps to have a dedicated board meeting or all-family retreat to discuss the options. The result from such a meeting ideally should be a written policy on board service, describing

In Their Own Words:

No Challenges in Your Family Foundation? Just Wait...

When I joined the Rasmuson Foundation, my work was limited to reviewing grant applications for the board. Family foundations 'issues'—like succession, geographic dispersion, donor intent—didn't concern the board or me. Guess what? They're ALL issues now. Amazing how quickly that happens. They are universal issues for family foundations. As a staff, the most challenging part of the job is to be in the role where you are not dominating, but facilitating the ability of the family to carry out their philanthropic goals.

—Diane Kaplan, Rasmuson Foundation

*The best policy is to **have** a policy.*

"We asked the six grandchildren to work out among themselves which three would be on the Board [in any given year]. It has always been easy."

—Jim Posner,
  Posner-Wallace Foundation

eligibility criteria, the process by which members are selected and the definition of their term limits. For examples of policies, such as selection criteria, term limits and rotation policies, see *Board Development and Structure*, pages 123–134.

The best policy for any board is to *have* a policy. Policies work best when they exist before a board is forced by circumstances to implement one, even if the pre-existing policy will require modification later on. If a board can anticipate changes (many of which are outlined in this book) and make basic decisions about how it will approach these issues, it will save the board from on-the-spot decisions that might later frustrate or alienate family members.

In Their Own Words:

Who Is Considered "Family" for Board Service?

"It is our policy to include all family members who want to participate in the foundation, so we knew the board was going to grow significantly bigger. Our children are now involved, and the farther we go from the original donor, the more tenuous it gets in managing the board. We have a geographically dispersed family, and the foundation is the only reason we all get together."

—Luther Tucker, Jr., Marcia Brady Tucker Foundation

"The Conrad N. Hilton Foundation limits its board membership to 11 seats. With such a large family, there is somewhat of a competition among family members for a seat. To address this, the Hilton board created a nominating committee which consists of three people. The board also does not allow trustees to retain life seats, thereby opening up slots for new members."

—Conrad Hilton, Jr., The Conrad N. Hilton Foundation

"The DeWitt and Caroline Van Evera Foundation board keeps a list of potential board candidates, which it reviews regularly. Currently, there are three possible successors from different family branches. The family is large but it is hard to find those who are interested in serving. We ask potential candidates to come observe our board meetings, and are working on a way to formally structure an orientation. To develop an orientation process, I began writing the history and mission and my experience with the foundation. I am the third generation of family trustees and my aunt, a second generation trustee, had written a chronological outline of foundation activity, which provides good background as I draft this orientation document. With a good orientation in place, we will share with new trustees what they can expect from the foundation, and what the foundation expects of them."

—Gretta Forrester, The DeWitt and Caroline Van Evera Foundation

"The basic challenge for the Posner-Wallace Foundation was how to bring in the third generation, without the first- and second- generation feeling outnumbered. Our consensus was to invite three of the grandchildren onto the board, and encourage all the others still to attend our meetings. The issue was how to select three individuals. Our solution was effective for everyone concerned: we asked the six grandchildren to work out among themselves which three would be on the board [in any given year]. It has always been absolutely easy and straightforward for them to decide, and has caused no bruised feelings."

—Jim Posner, Posner-Wallace Foundation

Size Does Matter

This Family Is Too Big

As a family grows over time, the board of the foundation often grows with it. Some families have found creative ways to include their increasing numbers and manage the growth, but in a large family the question will arise: how many is too many? For a board with many members vying to become involved, this can be tricky. The board may not want to exclude anyone, but it must also be sure its size doesn't become unmanageable.

An unwieldy board may frustrate participants by:

- Working against a donor's intent to provide a meaningful philanthropic experience that unifies the family and ensures the foundation's future.

- Being more time-consuming and expensive to administer. Costs include expenses such as board member travel for attending meetings, copying and mailing materials, conference and workshop registration fees for professional development, etc.

- Requiring additional foundation staff to deal with the volume and flow of board and committee activities and logistics.

This Family Is Too Small

Family foundation boards average six or seven people. Most states mandate a minimum size for corporate boards, generally three, but trusts may have as few as one trustee. A board might be extremely small, perhaps consisting of the original donor couple and no one else. Or, it may consist of the donor, one or two other family members, and a trusted advisor such as the family attorney. While there are few restrictions, small boards—or small families—might face a challenge if they wish to continue the family foundation over time. For example, what if the donor couple has no children to inherit the foundation, and no potential successors in the extended family? Who will run the foundation after the donors have died?

There are other disadvantages that may arise with small boards, even before the original donors have died. Small boards may:

- Become insular, lacking the breadth and depth of experience, perspective and judgment needed for informed, effective governance

- Force the foundation to look to paid advisors for assistance with management and compliance with foundation law, raising the cost of operations

- Work against genuine consensus because too few voices exist for broad discussions and mediation of disagreements.

Carefully Recruit New Board Members

Too often, boards rush to fill vacant spaces without thinking about the qualities they need in a new board member. When recruiting new members, be they family or not, a board can work strategically to identify and invite individuals to serve because of their skills and resources. Assess the individual's potential as an effective board member. Creating a job description for board members and eligibility requirements helps, as this makes clear what is expected from a new member and what that new member can expect. A well-thought-out recruitment process can also alleviate tension among family members by making decisions more objective and less personal—for example, if the board chooses one sibling over another for board membership.

To ensure a good fit, consider a trial period as part of the recruitment policy. Invite potential board members to serve temporary terms—such as an initial, one-year term—preceding full appointment.

Including Nonfamily Members

Many family foundation boards treasure the opportunity to practice their unique, family-centered brand of philanthropy. Yet, nonfamily board members can bring a wealth of knowledge, skills and professionalism that the foundation might not otherwise gain from a family-only pool. Even for foundations where size isn't an issue, board members recognize how often nonfamily members elevate the tenor of board meetings, either from their expertise in a funding area or their professional experience.

Whether or not there are family members to join the board, adding nonfamily members to the foundation board may be the best option. Nonfamily members add an element of neutrality if and when family dynamics come into play. Just as when there are invited guests at the dinner table, families tend to behave better around the board table when nonfamily members are present. Including nonfamily board members creates an environment of mutual consideration, says one family board member. "Simply put, family members act better around people they respect."

Including nonfamily members as decisionmakers also can be a healthy option as family size dwindles. Consider the benefits of all-family boards versus those with some nonfamily members:

Benefits of All-Family Boards:

- **Legacy.** The foundation is created as an intimate expression of a family's values or as an extension of its traditions of philanthropy.

- **Family unity.** A foundation may unify a family by providing a worthwhile common enterprise that brings a dispersed family together or binds it over generations.

- **Confidentiality or loyalty.** When foundation operations are viewed as offering a window into a prominent family's affairs, the option of all-family control may be appealing.

Benefits of Adding Nonfamily Board Members:

- **New voices.** Outsiders bring new energy, skills and expertise to enhance existing capabilities within the family.

- **Community perspective.** Nonfamily members can bring a community perspective or subject matter expertise to the foundation mission, its daily operations and changing circumstances.

- **Improved productivity.** With nonfamily members at the board table, family members are more likely to leave personal baggage at home, making for more productive and professional meetings.

Considering bringing on nonfamily board members? See the *Sample Discussion Worksheet* on page 134.

COLLEAGUE STORIES:
Family and Nonfamily, Equal Partners

Some family foundations wish to preserve the unity of an all-family governing structure, while others feel limited by it. The Jessie Smith Noyes Foundation is one example of a foundation that made the transition from an all-family board to including nonfamily members.

The Noyes Foundation maintained an all-family board for more than 20 years before realizing that it needed a broader pool of expertise and perspectives. Like many family foundations, it faced the problem of sustainability as the first generations of board members aged. So it began a long process of building a professional staff and a larger, more varied board.

Because it had no restrictions regarding board composition (except for a size limit of no more than 25 people), the foundation created a board with ideological, gender, racial, ethnic and skill diversity. The foundation also sought individuals with experience in the nonprofit sector to serve on the board. To encourage family involvement in the foundation's governance, each branch recommended a nonfamily representative to serve on the board. Now, the two first-generation family members serve for life, while all other board members serve six-year terms, as stipulated in the bylaws. A nonfamily member often chairs the Noyes Foundation board.

COLLEAGUE STORIES:
Merging Foundations

A foundation may merge with another for a number of reasons—to create a stronger, larger foundation, to reduce administrative costs, or to share resources and collaborate on funding areas. A foundation might also decide to merge when there is no one in the family to take over and the board wants to continue the work of the foundation.

For the Charles E. Culpeper Foundation, a 59-year-old private foundation in Stamford, Connecticut, the decision to turn its assets over to another private foundation required much thought and concern. The donor died in

---

Bringing on Board Members?
Use Normal Precaution

When a foundation adds a new board member or gives responsibilities to someone outside or even within the family, it should exercise normal caution. The board should perform background checks for every potential trustee, usually by a nominating committee. At a minimum when bringing on members, the board should check references and provide the new member with a letter of appointment that details all expectations and limitations.

Families should proceed slowly before turning over major responsibilities to any individual board member. It is the board's fiduciary responsibility to share control of the foundation instead of handing control of any or all aspects to one individual.

For more information, read *Governance: Family Foundation Library series*, Council on Foundations, 1997. To order, call 888/239-5221 or visit www.cof.org.

1940 and there was no family to carry it on. When the CEO thought about his own retirement, he also questioned who would succeed him. The board was quite small and several of the members had recently retired. With no obvious heir to take on the leadership, the Culpeper trustees chose to find another charitable entity to manage the legacy instead of closing it down or seeking a new generation of management.

In May 2002, Culpeper merged with the Rockefeller Brothers Fund (RBF) of New York City. The decision followed a year of conversations between the institutions' boards, made smoother by the fact that Colin Campbell, vice chairman of Culpeper's board, also happened to be president of the RBF. According to Benjamin Shute, RBF secretary, RBF seized the opportunity to review and consolidate its own funding areas, developing a new program architecture. This review and consolidation after the merger was motivated by the events of September 11, 2001 and by the decline in the value of RBF's endowment.

Through the merger, four Culpeper trustees came onto the RBF board and became full voting members. RBF also absorbed some of Culpeper's staff to assist with the transition and carry out Culpeper's programs. According to Shute, "Although it was a pretty smooth transition, it was not seamless. There was some reconciling of how the different board and staff members approached the work."

Shute gives this advice to other foundations considering mergers, "It is very important that boards spend time talking to one another and gain a common understanding about how it will go. Foundations also should bring staffs together in advance as well, encouraging them to think and talk about differences in how they operate."

"The two most important elements in any transition," maintains Shute, "are time and talk."

_____

COLLEAGUE STORIES:
Newsletters Help Large Families Keep in Touch

Family newsletters can be an excellent way to keep the family in touch and involved in philanthropy. The Andrus Family Philanthropy Program (AFPP), conceived by the Surdna Foundation and the extended Andrus family, keeps its more than 300 family members educated and involved through an annual newsletter called *Concinnity*, which is the family's special name for its five reunions held since 1973. Board and family members write feature stories of the five family philanthropies and short items that highlight a variety of volunteer opportunities. The *Doers* column, in particular, recognizes family members from every generation who have given of themselves and their time. "The newsletter is an excellent tool for providing awareness, education, and in some cases, opportunities to participate in the family's philanthropic work," said AFPP Executive Director Steve Kelban. "Its stories keep people connected and gives them a better picture of each of the family philanthropies." To view an issue of *Concinnity*, visit www.affund.org/andrus_library.htm.

TOOL BOX:
Family Involvement

Questions to Think About

- Does everyone understand the mission of the foundation?
- Are people in the family excited about the foundation's work?
- Does the foundation have an organizational structure that is effective and efficient enough to sustain it in the future?
- How does the board currently identify and recruit new members?
- Does the board have trouble selecting new board members? Why?
- What are the eligibility criteria for board membership?

FOR BOARD DISCUSSION:
Three Steps to Selection Criteria

Step One: Define Family
Who constitutes family for purposes of appointment to the board?

- Lineal descendants only?
- Spouses? What happens in the event of divorce?
- Domestic partners?
- Adopted children? Stepchildren? Their descendants?

Step Two: Define Who Else Can Serve on the Board

What are the criteria for board service?

- Should the board be open to those beyond the family? Why or why not?

- If we choose an all-family board, how can we bring community perspectives to the board?

- How do we gather expertise in the subject areas that we fund?

Step Three: Determine Eligibility Criteria

- What criteria do we use to select from among those eligible for board service? (For example, education level, volunteer service, philanthropic training such as conference attendance, service on a junior board, etc.)

- Do we want minimum or maximum ages for board service?

- What would constitute grounds for removal from the board?

Step Four: Define Terms and Rotation Policies

- Should we have term limits? If yes, how long should each term be?

- Should we limit the number of terms? The number of consecutive terms?

- Should we have a rotation policy? How many terms on and off should a board member serve?

For sample definitions of family, board criteria and term/rotation policies, see *Board Development and Structure,* pages 123–134 and *Sample Term Limit and Rotation Policy* on page 132.

BOARD MEMBERSHIP STRUCTURE:
A Tiered Approach

There are many ways to structure a board, depending on the number of seats available and the number of qualified people available and interested in serving.

One way to include the voices of new members (particularly nonfamily) is to use a membership structure of governance. This structure includes two tiers of power and responsibility. The first tier—usually reserved for a few senior family members—establishes the foundation's mission, makes policy decisions and appoints other members and directors to the foundation, who are often given term limits. This tier communicates the roles and responsibilities, as well as the foundation's values, to the directors. The first tier can remove directors who are ineffective. The second tier—the directors—votes on grant proposals and budgetary issues. Some family foundations even add an additional tier—the associates—often comprised of the younger generation, who are allowed to participate in meetings but not allowed to vote.

Here are the pros and cons of a tiered membership structure:

Pros:

- Opens seats on the board for new members while limiting board size

- Lets family maintain control of the foundation while involving nonfamily voices

- Grooms younger generation for service in a meaningful but limited way

- Defines roles of board members further as determined by tier

- Relieves the tension of imposing term limits on donors or family members who wish to serve life appointments.

Cons:

- May create resentment among tiers

- May concentrate too much power in members who have the authority to seat and remove board members.

For sample criteria for this type of membership structure, see *Sample Membership Structure: The Two-Tiered Board*, page 131.

TERM AND ROTATION POLICIES:
How Long Should Board Members Serve?

Once the board establishes selection criteria for board membership, it should consider term and rotation policies for board members. Family foundations are far less likely than other types of foundations to have term limits for board service— only 35 percent limit service for some or all board members. In comparison, 93 percent of community foundations limit board service.

There are many options for customizing these policies. Because of the flexible nature of family foundations, members can choose what resonates with the board. Here are some pros and cons of term and rotation policies:

Pros:

- Opens seats on the board for new members while managing board size

- Keeps board perspective from getting stale

- Gives many members in a large family an opportunity to serve

- Makes room for the voices of younger family members

- Provides a tactful way to remove ineffective board members

- Reduces board member burnout.

Cons:

- Removes the privilege of life membership on the board

- Forces experienced and valued board members to step down unnecessarily

- Requires hard work to regularly interest, recruit and orient new members.

If the foundation is hesitant to establish terms and rotation policies, but wants to bring fresh voices to the table, it might consider awarding the donors or other distinguished former board members an "emeritus" or "honorary" status. Members may remain on the board but in a nonvoting capacity. This position thanks them for their work and gives them an opportunity to continue on the board, while opening new seats. But this type of recognition should be used sparingly. The board needs to guard against becoming too big for effective discussions. It can also be hard to forge new directions with former leaders still at the table.

For a sample term and rotation policy, see *Sample Term Limit and Rotation Policy*, page 132.

MERGING:
Tips for Making a Smooth Transition

Thinking about merging with another organization? Even the best-planned merger can take its toll on a foundation board and staff. It can take up to three years for a merger transition to feel complete. Often it takes time for the organization's new combined board and staff to work through one or two major issues—or even a crisis—together, learning each other's work styles and creating a new way of doing things. Here are some ideas to help the merger process:

- Be sure to create a written agreement between parties, with help from an attorney

- Hold a retreat at the start of a merger to break the ice and talk about the new vision for the foundation

- Discuss the opportunities that a merger can bring for the foundation and for individuals

- Make clear the expectations, roles and responsibilities for all parties

- Create new job descriptions for board members and staff members

- Conduct regular meetings to monitor all aspects of the merger, including general office operations, costs, program areas and human resource issues

- Keep communication consistent and open.

Succession

For most family foundations, one of the biggest concerns is how to pass on leadership to the next generation. In a recent Council on Foundations *Foundation Management Survey*, three-quarters of respondents listed succession as the main issue facing their foundation. Yet, only one-third were doing anything to ready younger family members for their future roles.

A family foundation that develops a succession plan early will see the practical benefits immediately and prevent family difficulties later. Such a plan allows members in waiting to prepare for service and, because in most families the number of eligible trustees is likely to grow, enables the board to anticipate and prepare for eventual selection. Without a plan, a family may select arbitrarily, causing resentment or frustration on the part of those not included. Young members of the family, for example, may be denied the opportunity to serve the foundation at a time when they are most likely to provide a source of vitality and renewal for the foundation.

"Son, you're old enough now to start taking
responsibility for your own actions as well as mine."

Family foundations use different methods to engage new generations. Some of these methods include:

- Inviting younger family members to meetings as observers
- Taking them on site visits to potential/existing grantees
- Providing for ongoing professional development through conferences and workshops
- Offering service on advisory committees of the board
- Inviting them to participate in a discretionary grants or matching gifts program
- Establishing a junior or adjunct board
- Offering them the position of nonvoting "trustee candidate" for one year
- Encouraging them to serve as fellows or interns at foundations or nonprofits
- Asking for their input on projects in their areas of interest and/or expertise
- Establishing a next generation fund or a philanthropy program for the younger generation.

In Their Own Words:

Instill the Spirit of Philanthropy...Early On

I found it a challenge to assume a leadership role in the Siragusa Foundation, particularly since I never had any philanthropic training and because there was never any clear idea about what it is that my family is supposed to be doing with our money. Because philanthropy was not a huge part of our lives growing up, the rest of my third generation peers do not entirely see it as their responsibility to preserve the legacy of our grandfather and our family's philanthropic efforts.

When I served on the board in the 1980s, it was difficult to feel a part of the second-generation dominated group. I was the only third-generation member, and I felt intimidated. My brother, sister and cousins were aware of this situation, and I believe it has kept them somewhat removed from the foundation's work. I now work hard to engage the third generation and their children.

When I accepted the position of executive director, I was told that a large part of my responsibility would be to increase the visibility of the foundation in Chicago and to continue to honor the legacy of my grandfather's extraordinary life. My experiences have given me an important insight about philanthropy: The single-most important aspect of preserving a family foundation over several generations is instilling the spirit and the practice of philanthropy in a younger generation as early as possible.

—*Irene Phelps, Executive Director, The Siragusa Foundation*

Resources

For help instilling philanthropic values in children, read:

- *The Giving Family: Raising Our Children to Help Others*, Council on Foundations, 2001. Order #822.
- *The Succession Workbook: Continuity Planning for Family Foundations*, Council on Foundations, 2000. Order #821.

To order, call 888/239-5221 or visit www.cof.org.

In Their Own Words:

View Service as an Opportunity, Rather than a Duty

Learning about the myriad ideas that are constantly unfolding in the nonprofit world makes grantmaking both a continuing education and an exhilarating experience. When young people sense this excitement they want to participate. There are a few specific ways to make entry into the foundation world more interesting, to inspire the young to "hit the ground running" and to become active, concerned trustees.

First, I would suggest that any foundation's program encourage proposals that truly address society's changing needs, including proposals that show a willingness to tackle the most challenging, and often controversial, issues. If a foundation requires each board member to *read* these proposals, as we do, the younger trustees will receive a unique education, one impossible to find anywhere else. They will feel the excitement of this kind of work. And they will take invaluable lessons about what's happening in the world back into their own professional and social lives.

Second, we have found that nonfamily trustees are an important influence on younger board members. We are fortunate to have several who are outstanding, people with enlightened minds and a wide range of experience who through their knowledge, humor and intelligence make our meetings stimulating experiences. These trustees are role models to whom we—young and old—look for ideas and guidance. It is vital to select trustees who can inspire and intrigue rather than put down and alienate the younger generation.

Finally, younger board members want to be listened to during decision-making discussions. Their views and concerns are often refreshing and bring new insights to a given problem. After all, it is *their* future that foundations must ultimately address.

I think the underlying task for older generations is to constantly challenge the young to view their service as an opportunity rather than a duty. We demand that they work hard and take their obligations seriously, and we afford them respect for taking on a serious challenge. At the same time, we want them to have some fun. At our foundation both generations are enjoying sharing "the torch"— stretching our minds to figure out how we can best use our resources to make the world a better place.

—Katharine B. Mountcastle, Trustee, Mary Reynolds Babcock Foundation

COLLEAGUE STORIES:
Taking the Next Generation on Tour

For its family reunion and 50th anniversary, the Western New York Foundation created a family booklet. Instead of focusing on the family history, this keepsake told the story of the nonprofits the foundation has helped since its inception. According to trustee Richard Moot, "We looked back over our 50 years and hired a writer to visit and interview each of the 12 major agencies we funded." The foundation then went a step further by hiring a video company to produce a film on the agencies. "We let the work we've done for 50 years or so speak for itself."

When it was time to introduce the next generation to the foundation's work, the board took all younger members, 21 years and older, on a bus tour to all of the grantee offices. "We found that the best way to introduce the next generation was not anything we could say, but what the agencies had to say," says Moot. "The next-generation members who are now trustees had a chance to hear not only from their fathers and grandfathers, but to hear from the agencies themselves about what the foundation meant to them."

The bus tour wasn't only beneficial to the next-generation members, says Moot, but also in building even better grantee relations. "The agencies were impressed we took the time to feature them in our 50th Anniversary booklet and to organize a tour. It was a positive experience for everyone involved."

TOOL BOX:
Succession

Questions to Think About

- Does the foundation have a sufficient pool of interested family members from which to draw to ensure the continuity of the foundation?

- Do those family members have time to devote to the foundation? Do they have the personal resources to participate or can the foundation afford to reimburse their expenses for their efforts?

- Does the board have a plan for educating the next generation of leaders?

- Are there means for the broader family to be aware of the foundation's work (e.g., newsletters or family-only websites)?

- Are children in the family raised to value volunteerism and giving?

- Are there ways for young people to get involved in the foundation's work prior to board service?

Successful Successors: Challenges in Each Generation

Getting ready to involve a new generation? Consider these challenges and desired characteristics provided by both senior-generation and next-generation family members:

What Do Seniors Look for in Successors?

- Sharing the values and the dreams

- Respecting what has been built and building upon it further

- Helping the senior generation redefine an ongoing contribution and role

- Being open and receptive to being coached and mentored

- Earning the right to be successors and to step forward to grab the reins

- Valuing stewardship over "ownership"

- Realizing that philanthropy is far more than giving money. For donors, it's about values, principles and vision.

What Does the Next Generation Look for in Their Role as Successors?

- Proving themselves with responsibility and authority

- Communicating on the same level with senior family members

- Developing leadership: What do I need to learn?

- Being challenged: Don't be afraid to push me

- Gaining support.

Adapted by the Council on Foundations from the Loyola University Next Generation Leadership Institute

Tips to Welcome the Next Generation

- Record the foundation's history on audio or videotape.

- Emphasize open communication and mentoring.

- Demonstrate that participation has a genuine purpose.

- Open board meetings to everyone and distribute minutes (either in hard copy or posted on a website).

- Reach out to distant family members through conference calls.

- Plan a family retreat to facilitate the succession process.

- Consider options such as junior boards or advisory boards. Think about instilling a "promotion track" to becoming a full board member.

- Use case studies and real-life experiences to educate future generations.

Geographic Dispersion

As foundations age and expand, they face many of the growing pains that families themselves do. Family foundations, however, undergo an additional challenge: to meet the emotional needs of the family and the operational needs of the foundation—not always an easy task.

Geographic dispersion is a change inevitably encountered by mature family foundations. As family members move to different parts of the country, and even the world, a host of questions arise. How can the foundation keep a scattered board in contact, interested and active when the foundation is centered hundreds of miles away?

"For us, geographic dispersion brought with it a loss of passion in board members," says Lynette Malinger, executive director of the Speh Foundation. "Reading the proposals where they didn't know the funding area or communities made people lose excitement. The family lives in other places and wants to focus on other ideas."

Other challenges of geographic dispersion can include the following:

- Serving a region where few family members now reside
- Creating a new mission for a foundation that engages and motivates family members living in different states, even different countries
- Bringing to the board third-, fourth- or fifth-generation family members who have no personal connection to the original donor, the funding area or the region
- Balancing a limited travel budget to schedule convenient and economical board meetings for members scattered across the country
- Removing funds from the foundation's core mission by establishing several discretionary funds in communities where family members live
- Jockeying among board members to change the mission in ways that would benefit projects in their own communities.

In spite of the challenges that physically scattered boards may face, some foundations find that geographic dispersion is an *opportunity* rather than a shortcoming. Some use it as a way to learn about new communities and focus areas. By giving individual board members a chance to get involved in their own locales, the entire board can benefit through a sharing process and site visits.

"We hope to make use of the geographic distance between our board members to give each an opportunity to participate in his or her community in both leadership and volunteer capacities," says Irene Phelps, executive director of The Siragusa Foundation. "This way, family members will be more excited about the possibilities of our family philanthropy."

It's true that geographically dispersed foundations may have to work harder to arrange meetings. They may have to reassess their mission more frequently or hold discussions on dividing grant allocations by location. They may even have to invite nonfamily members onto the board to keep contacts in the original donor's hometown. However, in working through such issues, family foundations can reap great rewards.

In Their Own Words:

How Foundations Can Bridge the Distance

The Helen Sperry Lea Foundation originated in Washington, DC. Eight years ago, when we were all on the eastern seaboard, it was easier for us to hold meetings and communicate regularly. Now, with my sister in California, me in Minnesota and my parents still in Washington, we have had to change our [governing] style to bridge the distance.

Our family board approached the challenge of geography in three ways:

1. Build a Website and the Board Will Come

First, we threw technology at the problem. We held conference calls, communicated by faxes, sent e-mails. Just recently, we integrated a secure website with a pass code, allowing board members to drop off and pick up documents.

In researching how to build a website for our purposes, I found many of my questions answered at Council on Foundations conferences, particularly the technology sessions. I bought a couple books and asked colleagues and friends to give me tips. I didn't worry about how attractive the site would be, but how well it functioned.

The website now serves as a virtual main office where all our transactions take place. However, it did take time for the board to get used to it. Although both my dad and mom are very game to learn about computers, it took some time for them as an older generation to prefer using the website over faxes and FedEx's, and about a year until they were fully comfortable. Much of their learning came from watching me use the computer and hands-on practice.

If I could do it over, I would give the board a more formal orientation to the website, perhaps a mini-workshop. One idea would be to place computers in different rooms of the house, and send each board member to their own room. This would take the actual distance out of the learning process, but demonstrate that 1,000 miles between board members can be irrelevant to good communication.

2. Educate and Cooperate

Second, we took a "divide and conquer" approach. As we spread to other cities, we found it opened us to different recipients and different projects we wanted to fund. Our funding interests have grown more diverse, and our mission has broadened in terms of content. As a result, not everyone is as heavily involved in every grant like we used to be. Now, we each specialize geographically, concentrating and managing our own local grants.

In doing this, however, we've sacrificed some sense of family atmosphere, where we all knew each other's projects intimately. Now we know the projects, but mostly on paper alone. To compensate for this, we hold family meetings to "Educate and Cooperate." At these meetings, each board member makes presentations about each grant. We also rotate our board meetings—about three or four per year—among different cities, giving us an opportunity to visit various funding sites as well. This brings back the feeling that the entire board is aware of and involved in all the projects.

3. Deadlines That Work

The third, and most simple, tool is to use deadlines. Our board explored enforcing deadlines as a way to keep everyone on track. Living far from one another, it's easy for tasks to become "out of sight, out of mind." At times, everyone tends to procrastinate. Therefore, we developed a mutual agreement for deadlines: If you don't respond by the agreed upon time, you forfeit your vote for the upcoming meeting, and your proposal won't be reviewed until the following meeting.

This agreement on deadlines works for our board, keeping us from putting things off. Deadlines aren't meant to be mean, but to keep things running efficiently. They also allow people to opt out, without guilt, if in fact they're too busy at any given time.

In sum, geography can indeed be a challenge for family foundation boards, but it doesn't have to be limiting. With simple tools in place, such as technology, education and deadlines, a dispersed foundation board may find that it still runs efficiently and successfully—if not more so.

—R. Brooke Lea, Helen Sperry Lea Foundation

Facing Forever: *Planning for Change in Family Foundations*

Making the Mission Possible: Should It Be Broad or Narrow?

In working with a board that is geographically dispersed, is it better to have a broad mission or a narrow one? Some believe that it's easier to have a narrow mission with a few funding areas and regions, while others say it helps to widen the focus to fund in communities where board members reside. Like many questions that arise in family foundations, there's no one, right answer. If a mission is too narrow, it might exclude family members from different states or those with different interests. On the other hand, a mission that's too broad may yield a scattered, low-impact grant-making program.

How should the board approach its mission statement? Here are some steps that may help:

- Establish the board's priorities
- Decide how important family unity is relative to the funding focus and donor intent
- Determine how these considerations balance with community needs
- Revisit the mission regularly.

Whatever a board decides, it should continually review the mission to monitor its effectiveness and maintain family investment in that mission. Many foundations hold regular retreats—yearly or biennially where family members explore their philanthropic interests and identify or reconnect to underlying shared values. The foundation can then use that information to write or revise missions and guidelines to which all board members subscribe.

"If a mission statement is too broad, it could cause conflict regarding interpretation. If a mission is too narrow, it might not interest board members across geography and generations. What's the answer?—A carefully crafted middle ground, rooted in the family's shared values and revisited on a periodic basis."

—Karen Green,
Managing Director,
Family Foundation
Services,
Council on Foundations

Using Technology

While technology is never a replacement for face-to-face communication, it helps foundations take care of routine business. Many boards use e-mail, the telephone and the Web to schedule and plan board meetings, keep members informed and even pre-screen proposals.

With board members spread across the country and the high costs of travel, more and more foundations are wondering if they can hold board meetings by conference calls. What's the advantage of using this technology? It makes it easier for members to participate. However, it reduces the personal interaction that brings a sense of cohesion and mutual understanding among board members.

Still, some boards decide to hold at least one of their board meetings by phone, to attract more participants and cut down on administrative expenses. If your foundation decides to hold a meeting by phone, check with your local telephone company to see what conferencing options it offers. You might consider a speaker phone called a conferencing unit for multiple users in the same room. These units are designed so that several people can easily hear and speak to callers without having to cluster around one telephone handset.

COLLEAGUE STORIES:
Private Sections on Foundation Websites

Private websites and e-mail can be valuable tools for the geographically dispersed board. These technology tools promote information exchange and often jump-start—and in some cases, replace—face-to-face board meetings. The Nord Family Foundation created a private section on its public website to keep its 30-plus family members informed and engaged in the foundation. Family members and trustees use passwords to access information on foundation operations, grant requests and resources. "Our ultimate goal," says John Mullaney, the foundation's executive director, "is to use this information for more informed trustee meetings, more responsible grantmaking and a clearer understanding of the administrative issues that staff and trustees must address." The site also features information, bylaws, committee tasks and a finance section.

In Their Own Words:

Ideas for Geographically Dispersed Family Foundations

Keep the Board Local

The Weiboldt Foundation averts the dilemma of geographic dispersion. Weiboldt funds in the Chicago area, and requires that its board members be residents of Chicago. If a board member moves from the Chicago area, he or she must step down from the board. This way, the foundation ensures that all board members have an interest in its regional funding. From the beginning, Weiboldt stores were local, and that has always been the focus."

—*John Darrow, Weiboldt Foundation*

Easy Ways to Stay in Touch

Our board is geographically dispersed. We have two board meetings per year, with dates set well in advance. Even so, unexpected events sometimes limit attendance. To keep good communication among board members, we use e-mail regularly and the telephone, although usually for one-on-one discussions instead of conference calls.

We also distribute our board book information on CD-ROM (printed for those who prefer).

—*Nathanael Berry, Sandy River Charitable Trust*

TOOL BOX:
Geographic Dispersion

Tools to Stay in Touch

- Revisit the foundation mission regularly, weighing how diverse family interests are impacting the foundation's effectiveness in achieving its central mission.

- Educate the family on the foundation's funding region, and if and why it was important to the original donor to focus funding in that region.

- Consider a donor-advised fund in the donor's hometown if family members no longer reside there.

- Offer limited discretionary grants or donor-advised funds that can be used by board members in their own communities.

- Become a national (or even international) grantmaker with no geographic restrictions.

- Plan board meetings to precede or follow family vacations, retreats or reunions.

Motivating the Board Across the Miles

How do family foundations keep board members on track, in spite of geographic sprawl? Here are some ideas:

- **Mission.** Periodically revisit the mission statement and guidelines as a board. Review for relevancy, donor intent, interest to current board and geographic funding limitations.

- **Location.** Rotate meetings and, if applicable, site visits to the different locations where board members live.

- **Work and Play.** Schedule board meetings back-to-back with family vacations or reunions (making sure expenses for each are clearly delineated).

- **Communication.** Keep it clear, concise and ongoing. Take advantage of technology.

- **Grants.** Allow board members to be creative and find on-mission grantees in their own backyards.

- **Education.** Inform and educate one another on funding areas and/or projects of individual interest.

- **Gentle persistence.** Make requests in advance and follow up on those requests in a patient, albeit persuasive, way.

- **Deadlines.** Incorporate deadlines and consequences for not meeting deadlines.

- **Resources.** Share summaries of conferences, workshops and publications to keep the board abreast of new developments in the field.
- **Professional development opportunities.** Offer board members the opportunity to connect with colleagues, share experiences and expand their knowledge of the field.

Chapter in Sum: Family Involvement

What Success Looks Like

All family foundations face family involvement challenges, based on family size, location and interest level. To keep members involved, a successful foundation has:

- Recruitment, selection and orientation practices
- A board membership structure, term limits and rotation policies
- A decisionmaking process based on preparation, not personality
- A plan followed by actions to engage the next generation
- A geographically dispersed family that commits to a common mission, is interested and engaged in the foundation, and meets face-to-face for board meetings.

"Before we begin this family meeting, how about we go around
and say our names and a little something about ourselves."

Chapter 2:
Dealing with Differences

In this chapter:

- Common Conflicts on Boards
- Why Discord Isn't Always Bad
- What Happens When…?
  - Divorce
  - Generations Disagree
  - Transfer of Leadership
  - Sibling Rivalry
  - Personal Issues
  - Troubled Board Members
  - Strained Relations Between Board and Staff
- Consensus-Building Strategies
- Consultant-Facilitated Retreats

Being a member of a family foundation can be rewarding. But because the work is ingrained within the family structure, it requires greater participation, commitment and patience from everyone involved. Nevertheless, misunderstandings and disagreements can occur.

Your board will need to distinguish between normal disagreements and inappropriate levels of conflict. Do your disagreements illuminate other members' views and generate good discussion? Or do they impede foundation performance? There may be no simple way to resolve the communication issues and tensions that challenge the effectiveness of your foundation. But members of family foundations should know that they are not alone in facing these challenges.

*"Take a load off, Leonard—we're watching
Generations X and Y duke it out."*

Conflict is a natural part of all human relationships and a dynamic in all group settings. If treated as an opportunity for growth and creativity, conflict can be a positive experience leading to great outcomes. Yet as a society and as individuals, we are not as comfortable managing conflict and using it for our benefit as we could be. For family foundations, it can be critical to develop conflict resolution skills in order to find balance between the professional and the personal.

Read this section to learn of some tools for dealing with differences and to see how your colleagues handled uncomfortable situations and found opportunities amid the challenges. Although the examples come from a diverse group of family foundations, most agree that working through disagreements has improved their philanthropy as well as their relationships with one another. And, as one trustee said, "In our family, it's our conflicts that have kept us sane."

Common Conflicts on the Board

Family relationships among board members can be both an asset and a challenge. Here are some potential conflicts that a family foundation board might encounter:

- Members of the younger generation have different interests than older members

- Founders have a hard time transferring leadership to the next generation

- New family members who join the board, such as spouses, do not share a common history with other members

- Board members persist in their roles as family members—even in the professional setting of board meetings

- Nonfamily board members or staff are drawn into unproductive family dynamics or are confused by them

- Family members who devote considerable time to the foundation resent those who participate only in board meetings, or vice versa

- Family members hold differing political or religious ideologies that affect funding decisions

- Family members have different funding and/or geographical interests that affect funding decisions

- Board member and staff member roles aren't well differentiated or understood.

"Families are hard to work with. We are trying to get away from the personal hurts and be more businesslike."

—Luther Tucker, Jr.,
Marcia Brady
Tucker Foundation

Why Discord Isn't Always Bad

Healthy dissent can actually help foundation boards thrive, as members challenge one another's assumptions, beliefs and funding priorities. Decisionmaking by consensus can be a useful tool, but if boards insist on 100 percent agreement, it may be at the cost of meaningful discussion.

Take, for example, the Posner-Wallace Foundation, which faces the unusual problem of a multi-generational board with *too* much consensus. "There is not enough conflict of the meaningful sort, where we engage in active interaction and must work through multiple preferences on which philanthropic direction to take," says Jim Posner, who recognizes that a time of dissent will probably come. "Our hope is that with a background of trying to listen to each other, the differences in our preferences will not fracture—but reinforce—the sense of mission."

According to Jeffrey Sonnenfeld in "What Makes Great Boards Great" (*Harvard Business Review*, September 2002), "The most effective boards may be those that are contentious, that regard dissent as an obligation and treat no subject as undiscussable." Boards should foster a culture of open dissent, probing silent members for their opinions and removing any pressure to conform to the majority.

In Their Own Words:

Learn More from Conflicts than Agreements

We don't pretend that our transition to an independent foundation from a family-run foundation was without conflict. But scholars are increasingly telling us that conflict, while sometimes painful, is necessary for the health of an organization. Too much unexamined consensus can reinforce "groupthink." In the absence of alternative views, we may ignore or caricature new ideas. Subtle pressures to conform may arise, silencing differences of opinion. We may overestimate our power, or the moral worthiness of our actions. We can fail to hold ourselves accountable to others who are affected by our decisions. Foundations like ours may learn more from conflicts than agreements.

Maybe the best measure of our foundation's health isn't how often we agree, but whether we are struggling with the most important questions of the time. These days, most of our debates are over strategies for preserving and improving the environment, about what a just society might look like, and about whether and how the market economy can be reconciled with the natural world and with democracy. We can't imagine having those debates within a narrow slice of society, because the answers will affect us all.

—*Edith Muma and Chad Raphael, The Jessie Smith Noyes Foundation*

COLLEAGUE STORIES:
Majority Rules

To work through conflicts, some families adhere to a "majority rule" policy. This can be very effective if the family members in the minority feel the board has seriously considered their point of view.

One example of a foundation that uses majority rule is the Harris and Eliza Kempner Foundation. When it came time for the board to discuss the funding of organizations that provide abortions, the large and diverse board of this $30 million family foundation in Galveston, Texas had strong and differing opinions on the subject. The family debated whether to adopt a policy stating that if "three or more board members disagree on whether or not to fund 'a moral issue,' then the foundation would not fund in that area." They voted the proposition down, deciding that the majority would rule. According to Executive Director Elaine Perachio, "The board was comfortable with this decision because people felt they had had their say. Family members have a high level of trust and affection for one another and don't take these decisions personally."

Frank Merrick of the Merrick Family Foundation believes that consensus voting can come at a cost to good grantmaking. "If families try to do everything by a consensus acclamation vote, that is minority rule," says Merrick. "If one person out of ten disagrees with a grant proposal and the proposal is tossed out, that is unhealthy. Boards should use majority rule, even if it means disagreements in opinion." For more on consensus building, see page 57.

In Their Own Words:

Changing the Role of the Family

As the Nathan Cummings Foundation matured, relationships among family members on the board were fraught with as many quirks and permutations, positive and negative, as in "real life"—with one huge difference: this family was engaged in the ongoing job of dispensing millions of dollars each year. "One of the challenges of a family foundation," asserts Ruth Durchslag, "is that it involves family relationships, and family relationships are, by nature, intense and complicated."

Working together with their parents on the board had enriched those fortunate enough to have done so. For James Cummings, working with his father, Herb, "was really the first time that we had ever been in some kind of collegial arrangement. Instead of being just father and son, we were now also two men dealing with issues of importance to us both." With his mother, Diane Cummings, on the board, Michael Zuieback found disagreements about issues "no different than when you sat around the dinner table and voiced opposing viewpoints."

—*Deborah Gardner,* The Nathan Cummings Foundation: Looking to the Future, Honoring the Past, *1997.*

In Their Own Words:

Orientation Can Prevent Misunderstanding

Our foundation invited a new board member who brought proposals that didn't fit the focus. She assumed the board would rubber stamp whatever proposal she brought before us. This is not how we operate, although to someone new it might have seemed that way. We had to keep rejecting her proposals, and she responded by resigning pleasantly from the board. In retrospect, we realized that we never gave her any orientation to the board or on our grantmaking procedures. If we had, we could have saved ourselves from some tension and misunderstanding.

—*Gretta Forrester, Trustee Advisor, DeWitt and Caroline Van Evera Foundation*

What Happens When...?

Divorce

Divorce is never easy for any family. Divorces that occur within family foundations where both spouses serve on the board have an added level of complexity. If a divorce occurs between the original donor couple, for example, which spouse will "get" the foundation? Or in another example, what happens in a divorce when a second-generation spouse is more active in the foundation than the family member?

No one wants to talk about the possibility of divorce. Yet, a board that prepares for such a circumstance can save itself tension and trouble in the future, should a divorce occur. Boards should discuss and create policy for what would happen in the case of divorce, ideally before any in-law comes on the board.

When going through a big transition such as a divorce, be patient.

COLLEAGUE STORIES:
A Family or Institutional Issue?

Divorces can range from amicable to litigious, and in the latter the most difficult time might be during or even before separation, long before divorce itself. John Darrow, president and fourth-generation member of the 80-year-old Weiboldt Foundation, went through a divorce several years ago.

According to Darrow, "Board membership could be an issue people might fight over in a divorce—it comes down to the most family[-sensitive] aspect of the board, when the board must look at the alternatives of how to deal with the situation at a time when emotions are raw." At the time of his divorce, his ex (who was an honorary board member at the time) stepped down from the board at his request. She is now involved in the field of philanthropy professionally.

In speaking about his work as a trust officer for Northern Trust Company, Darrow says, "One client is very amicable with the ex-spouse, but there are others who wouldn't be in the same room. It is important not to let divorce impact the ongoing work of the foundation. The leadership should figure out the best course of action. In most cases, I imagine the board would ask the nonfamily member to leave—sometimes well before the divorce."

Darrow says a pre-written policy on board eligibility in the event of divorce may help, but even that may come too late. "I agree that the issue should be discussed before an in-law comes on to the board, but I don't see how a policy can effectively anticipate the range of issues. To me, each family board is probably a unique mix of family gathering and business institution. The trick is trying to use the strengths of each facet to overcome the problems presented. Divorce is a situation where you have to emphasize the family aspect more than the institutional."

"Hey, what if marriages had term limits?"

COLLEAGUE STORIES:
Divorce Leads to a New Foundation

Pat Stryker was the original donor to the Stryker/Short Foundation that she and her husband formed in 1996. At the time of their divorce, the Stryker/Short Foundation terminated and rolled its assets into the Bohemian Foundation, with a new mission and vision. The structure of the board changed quite a bit as well. The current board consists of Pat Stryker and her children (two from a previous marriage, and one from her marriage with Short), and an advisory board with a few of the original board members.

According to Bohemian's former grants manager Beth Stipe, the transition was frustrating at times. "Pat did a lot of talking with others and soul searching to rediscover her direct passions, outside of her previous relationship. She needed a process to put those passions into a form all her own." The foundation hired outside consultants who held several retreats, reviewed the vision, goals, and strategies of the foundation and held meetings with individual board members. "It helps to bring in qualified consultants to do due diligence and research. Consultants should have foundation experience and fit personally with those involved as well."

Beth's advice to others going through a similar transition is to be patient. "It is a long process. Most people don't make a foundation overnight, or go through a divorce quickly. You can't expect that big a change in such a short time."

Generations Disagree

Power struggles between generations are common, with or without family foundations. Older family members have stature, experience and power that they may not want to relinquish. Younger generations have fresh ideas and want the authority to put them in action. The older generation may believe the younger one is inexperienced, immature or unmotivated. The younger generation may believe the older one is patronizing, domineering or stodgy. Typically, truth and distortion exist on both sides.

Katherine Mountcastle of the Mary Reynolds Babcock Foundation spoke of her own experience of generations growing together, noting that the younger generation in her foundation brought sophistication and insight to the board. "If the older generations were willing to listen to the younger ones, and willing to make constructive change, there was little conflict," says Mountcastle. "The older people have to learn to give up some of that power and listen to the younger generation."

Donors with strong entrepreneurial personalities often have the greatest difficulty relinquishing control, especially when, wittingly or unwittingly, they regard the foundation as an extension of themselves. Sometimes the next generation may not be ready because they never had a chance to try. The result is that after the donor dies, the successors either flounder, not knowing what to do, or follow the ways of their predecessors.

COLLEAGUE STORIES:
Founder's Fund

Sometimes the older generation will say they want to transfer some or all of the grantmaking authority, but are unable to let go. The Atkinson Foundation faced such a struggle. According to administrator Betty Curtis, the first-generation founder had difficulty disengaging from the foundation. Even after he brought his sons onto the board, the founder would repeatedly override their decisions. The foundation's solution? The board established a Founders Fund—a discretionary amount over which the founder had complete control—while the rest of the grantmaking budget was handled by the next generation. As Curtis says, "If you want kids to play in the sandbox, you've got to give them some sand." The original founder is now gone, but the fund for his two sons still exists.

> *"If you want kids to play in the sandbox, you've got to give them some sand."*
>
> —Betty Curtis, Atkinson Foundation

COLLEAGUE STORIES:
Generational Splits

Some foundations choose to split along generational lines for reasons other than disagreements. In the following example, a separate foundation formed as a learning tool for younger members.

The Klingenstein Third Generation Fund, established in 1993, began as a seed grant from the family foundation. According to executive director Sally Klingenstein, "It is a small fraction of what the main fund is worth. It didn't separate us from the main fund per se, but allowed us to have our own vehicle to express ourselves and learn on our own. We never thought of it as a split, but as an educational vehicle."

In the 1980s, Klingenstein's father was the president of the foundation her grandfather started. There were eight people on the board—her cousins, siblings, father and uncle. Her father and uncle would inform the younger generation what was going on with the foundation. "They weren't ready to give us any kind of voice," said Klingenstein, even though her siblings and cousins were all in their 30's at the time.

The third generation asked the father and uncle for some money ($5 million compared to the main fund's $100 million) to start their own foundation. "That way, we could prove that we will one day be ready to take the main fund over, while creating our own funding areas and making a mark," Klingenstein said.

"We used the main fund as a model, since it was a top-notch example to follow," said Klingenstein. Even so, the third generation doesn't plan to merge back into the main fund, but leave it for the following generation. According to Klingenstein, "We've been able to maintain harmony by doing it this way and we plan to continue to use it as a way to train successive generations."

Transfer of Leadership

When a foundation undergoes a transfer of leadership, it may be difficult for the founder to let go of authority. Typically called *founder's syndrome*, this commonly occurs when the foundation operates according to the personality of a prominent person in the organization—for example, the original donor or board chair/president. The founder may think of the foundation as "his" or "hers," rather than a public trust governed by the board to benefit a greater community.

Founder's syndrome can result in a number of challenges, some of which include:

- Increased turnover of board and staff members
- The foundation struggles from one crisis to the next
- Next generation board members feel they don't have a voice
- Board members become afraid of the founder.

No founder sets out to damage the foundation, and often the founder doesn't realize the negative effects of his or her behavior. Eventually, most realize they must change the way they operate and learn to develop a more inclusive leadership style. Until that time, there are actions board members can take to alleviate the stress related to founder's syndrome.

"Sorry, Pop, but your message is no longer relevant to the younger audience."

COLLEAGUE STORIES:
All In The Name of the Founder

The Foss Foundation exemplifies the classic struggle between generations. In 1985, when Julian Foss was 73 years old, he set up a family foundation in Phoenix, Arizona. At the time, his four children were in their 30's and 40's. Foss invited only one, his third child—a son—to serve on the board. The foundation operated without a formal mission statement, funding various organizations at Foss's whim. When his son realized that his father wanted him only to rubber-stamp his decisions, he quit the board. Foss's daughter, Julie Stuhr, was eager to participate in the foundation; however, her father pointedly ignored her requests to serve.

In the spring of 1993, her father reintroduced the subject of the children's role in his foundation, but vacillated about their readiness. This time, the siblings responded in a new way: they enrolled in a workshop offered by their local regional association of grantmakers and began exchanging information among themselves. "We wanted to show our father that we respected his wishes," said Stuhr, "but we also decided to work together as a family."

> —*Excerpt from "The Truth About Succession Planning," by Deanne Stone,* Foundation News & Commentary, *January/February 1994.*

Sibling Rivalry

Rivalry is built into sibling relationships from an early age. This rivalry can continue well into adulthood and manifest itself in long-standing rifts among entire family branches. Kept within boundaries, sibling rivalry can be productive to an extent, motivating siblings to excel in their work and gain respect for one another. When siblings have a history of competition, however, it can affect foundation performance.

The form that this rivalry takes depends on, among other things, age, personality, success in personal and professional lives, and whether the parents serve on the board. Siblings are especially sensitive to unequal treatment—either real or perceived—causing emotions to erupt around the board table. If rivalry isn't dealt with in a responsive and realistic way, it can disrupt the grantmaking process, interfere with foundation operations and—in the worst-case scenario—cause the family foundation to split into different branches.

In Their Own Words:

Founder's Syndrome

Although my family foundation has been around since 1950, philanthropy was not a large part of my life growing up. My grandfather started the foundation, and for a long time it only funded organizations with which he had some sort of personal connection or involvement. In a way, the foundation suffered for many years from "founder's syndrome," and by this I mean that my grandfather didn't have a particular, narrowly defined philanthropic vision. Board members learned more about rubber-stamping grant proposals from a wide range of unconnected organizations that inevitably had ties to my grandfather than they did about exploring their own philanthropic interests.

—*Irene Phelps, Executive Director, The Siragusa Foundation*

COLLEAGUE STORIES:
When Family Branches Divide

In the Archie D. and Bertha H. Walker Foundation, six children of the donors originally ran the foundation in the 1970s. As the third generation came of age, the second generation reinforced the divisions among themselves by recruiting their children to the board to form voting blocs.

David Griffith, the former president of the board, recounts: "The grantmaking meetings were like political battles, and proposals were tagged by branches. Trustees would make indirect attacks on one another and then stonewall, trying to wear down their opponents. The third generation got tired of being pulled into their parents' arguments, and some of them quit the board or moved out of town. The second generation called a family meeting to discuss the future and even whether they should continue as a family foundation. They each expressed their desire to maintain family control, but recognized that, if they were to hold the family together, they would have to find new ways of conducting business."

The board took two steps toward that goal. They brought in a consultant to coach trustees on improving their communication skills, and they developed specific policies and guidelines covering everything from board nominations and grantmaking procedures to codes of conduct, which they then all agreed to abide by. "Over the year of working with the consultant on communication, we learned how to disagree with one another without personalizing our differences—a real breakthrough,"

"We learned how to disagree with one another without personalizing our differences."

—David Griffith

continues Griffith. "We also attended workshops and seminars to help us understand our own behavior and our family dynamics. The result is that now we're much better at identifying clash-points and at separating the proposal from the person supporting it."

—*Partial excerpts from* Family Issues: Family Foundation Library series, *by Deanne Stone, Council on Foundations, 1997*

"...family members come together for a purpose that takes them outside of themselves."

—Helene O'Neil Cobb

In Their Own Words:

Families Should Embrace Differences

All parents want their children to get along. Unfortunately, parents cannot guarantee this, and the creation of a family foundation cannot make this happen. (Is it ever appropriate for a parent donor to expect, rather than merely hope, that ensuing generations will continue to work together as a family?) Family foundations, however, can foster togetherness by providing opportunities for real growth and learning, as family members come together for a purpose that takes them outside of themselves. A family that embraces its differences and appreciates the contributions of diverse family members is more likely to succeed as a family foundation *and* as a family. By giving each generation and family branch the opportunity to bring its myriad talents and interests into the life of the foundation and make its own contributions to the world of philanthropy, the family foundation is more likely to survive. Such simple generosity and inclusiveness would help more families to survive too.

—*Helene O'Neil Cobb, "Family Foundation Feuds," Foundation News and Commentary, January/February 2001*

Personal Issues

In a family foundation setting, emotional issues are likely to come to the front. These issues may stem from individual differences among members, an individual's relationship to wealth and family, or the delicate challenge of getting along with others—especially loved ones.

The following are a few scenarios of how personal issues may affect family and foundation relationships. One thing board members might remember is that personal issues are inevitable in any group endeavor. When acknowledged and properly dealt with, these issues needn't derail the foundation's work, and in fact, they may lead the organization in new directions.

Individual Differences

Disagreements may have nothing to do with power struggles between generations or family branches, but rather with individual differences between two or more family members. Everyone has his or her own ideology, interests, communication style and personality. These differences are positive and important—they enable people to learn new perspectives and gain respect for other beliefs. Yet, individual differences are often tied to personal values, which can lead discussions into deeper, more emotional disputes. Individual differences come in many forms including religion, politics and funding priorities.

Privacy

Some family members are embarrassed by their involvement with a foundation. They may not feel comfortable being seen as "wealthy" when the money was earned by the founder. Moreover, they may not be wealthy, even though they serve on a family foundation with large assets. Perhaps they aren't comfortable with the image that comes with being associated with the foundation and worry that friends will see them as different. In some extreme cases, they might worry for their safety and that of their children. This concern for privacy may affect how the individual responds and communicates with others on and off the board.

Whose Money Is It?

Sometimes family heirs have a difficult time understanding why a donor would leave a large part of the estate to the foundation, as opposed to individual family members. They may feel slighted or believe that the prior generation was not concerned with their future or lacked faith in their judgment. If heirs have struggled financially or if there exists a large economic gap among family members, this can create difficult emotional circumstances.

In this situation, it may ease the difficulties if heirs remember that more than half of the corpus of the foundation would likely have been paid in taxes had it not been for the establishment of the foundation, that the donor viewed the funding of the foundation as a worthy endeavor and that they are charged with governing an important public trust.

Self-Worth

Sometimes, an heir has grown up under the influence of a strong and directing parent, who imposed expectations and standards of conduct. If the heir has had few independent experiences, few opportunities to fail and few unsupervised successes, he or she will find it difficult to possess a feeling of personal worth. This self-perception may be reflected in the heir's dealings with money, his or her interpersonal relationships and level of involvement in foundation operations.

COLLEAGUE STORIES:
A Matter of Politics

When the Jacobs family formed a foundation in 1989, they held very different political views. These different views grew into battles over philosophy and methodology and what the mission should be. Those arguments ceased on the day that they decided to fund microenterprises, which fit into Joe Jacobs' entrepreneurial philosophy and his daughters' interests in issues of poverty and empowerment. As the family members became immersed in their research, their political differences took second place to the excitement of the larger project. "At the beginning we were more entrenched in our separate views," says Linda. "We used to argue over whose politics were more compassionate. Now we're more flexible and forgiving. When you share the same goals, it's easier to ascribe compassion to the other side." If anything, slugging out their political differences has brought this family closer together.

—*Excerpt from* Family Issues: Family Library series,
   by Deanne Stone, Council on Foundations, 1997

Troubled Board Members

Debate among board members is often a healthy way to illuminate differences and improve operations. Debate isn't always healthy, however, when repeatedly caused by a troubled board member.

Sometimes family members have personal issues that affect the way they relate to the rest of the board. Personal issues may be rooted in their involvement with the foundation or the wealth itself and may include:

- Lack of self-worth
- Resentment of the donors or other board members
- Embarrassment or guilt associated with the wealth
- Feelings of entitlement.

Regardless of the root cause, a troubled board member can bring unseen problems to a family foundation, limiting successful communication and, at times, even thwarting operations. Troubled board members might:

- Spread misinformation, either unintentionally or deliberately
- Send mixed messages or take contradictory positions
- Repeatedly disrupt or manipulate the flow of discussion
- Stifle other members' ideas or contributions
- Verbally attack other members or give some "the silent treatment"
- Cause the board or staff to alter its style of operation to accommodate his or her troublesome behavior.

Family foundation boards should be prepared to address the problems caused by a troublesome board member. Taking preventive measures in advance can help foil future problems.

In Their Own Words:

Dealing with a Disruptive Board Member

My brother got in some trouble a few years ago, costing himself two years in jail and costing the family a lot of money. In spite of this, the family gave him a seat on the board to honor the wishes of my father, who, as he was dying, asked that my brother be offered the opportunity to be involved in the foundation. In response to this situation, the board devised new bylaws to protect itself from this potentially troublesome family member as best we could.

For example, we changed the amount of time it takes for a new member to come onto the board. Where previously it took one year, we changed the bylaws to 18 months, prolonging when my brother could actually come into service. We also instilled a one-year term limit for all family members and added a rule that the board must vote if a member wishes to renew his or her term. We made it clear that being on the board is not a birthright—if a member fails to get along or misses meetings or asks us to do something inappropriate, the board has the authority to ask that person to step down from service. As a reminder of the laws, we read the conflict of interest statement at the start of every meeting and always placed it behind the agenda in our board meeting booklets.

To plan ahead for a possible removal, we designated a nonfamily member as chair of the nominating committee. That way, if we ever have to remove a family member from the board, the responsibility falls into the hands of a nonfamily member as opposed to family.

In talking with others, it seems that many family foundations put up with disruptive family members longer than they should. For other foundations in a similar situation, I would recommend spending more time with the troubled member. This may avoid uncomfortable situations in the future. For example, my brother at one point tried to get us to do something for his own personal benefit. He did not understand the third-party disqualified person rule. Had we as a board given a better orientation to him, this tense situation could have been averted.

I would also recommend spending more time with the other trustees to see how they really feel as a result of the disruptive member. Our family is polite—we don't talk bad about each other in person, but we do behind each other's backs. By talking honestly to one another about how this was affecting the board, we may have offered a higher level of support through a tough situation. What helped us through was that we all want to love each other at the end of the day. Not all families are like that.

—Anonymous

Strained Relations Between Board and Staff

Typically, when family foundations reach a certain size or age, they consider hiring staff. Often, this can bring an enormous transition to the foundation, as both board and new staff juggle roles. The transition can be particularly difficult for board members who have served as unpaid managers for many years; although they may not want the continued responsibility of staffing the board, they may want to maintain the ownership of the work.

The best way to circumvent this dilemma is to make board and staff roles clear before interviews even begin. Written job descriptions for both board and staff can be a good tool for this. For a sample job description, see *Sample Board Member Job Descriptions*, pages 136 and 137.

TOOL BOX:
Dealing with Differences

Questions to Think About

■ When conflict erupts in the boardroom, what are the causes?

■ How does the board react to conflict, in and out of the boardroom?

■ How does the staff (if any) react to conflict, in and out of the boardroom? What tools do they use to work around the conflict and/or attempt to mediate?

■ Has the foundation discussed splitting, spending down, or terminating as a result of conflict?

■ Does everyone on the board have an equal voice? If not, how does that affect the way the foundation is run? How might all voices be heard?

■ Who (really) runs the foundation—a particular member, board or staff? Are you comfortable with the balance?

■ What tools has your foundation used to build consensus? Among generations? Among board and staff? Among family branches? Have these efforts been successful?

Orient New Board Members Early On

Becoming a board member can be a complex and confusing experience, for both family and nonfamily members. Foundations should give new members a road map—an orientation that describes their legal, financial and grantmaking roles and responsibilities, as well as a history of the foundation and its values. A good orientation can prevent problems. Orientation training can take many forms:

■ A briefing by the board chair or team of veteran board members

■ An extended mentoring experience where a new board member "shadows" an existing board member, attending meetings and site visits

■ A "foundation history" tour, visiting sites important to the family legacy (e.g., factory, neighborhood) and/or locations the foundation has funded

■ A formal group training presented by a consultant hired by the foundation

■ A presentation with relevant resource materials prepared by foundation staff.

Whether orientation is a one-time briefing or, ideally, a continuing education for all board members, an essential tool is a basic board handbook. Such a book will serve as an excellent resource during orientation and throughout the board member's tenure.

Here are some items to include in the **board orientation handbook**:

■ **Foundation purpose**—mission, vision, and values statements; history; donor intent letter; description of grantmaking process and guidelines; long-range plan, and most recent annual report.

■ **Board membership and calendar**—list of board member names and contact information, job descriptions of chair and members, committee lists, and calendar of meetings.

■ **Bylaws and policies**—articles of incorporation and bylaws; board policies on indemnification and on directors' and officers' liability insurance; conflicts of interest; and attendance, compensation and/or expense reimbursement policies.

■ **Staff (if any)**—staff names, job descriptions, and personnel policies.

■ **Finance**—investment policy and reports, budget, audit statement, and financial procedures.

■ **Minutes and issues**—minutes of recent board meetings, description of current issues for discussion, and a sample meeting agenda.

From The Family Advisor: Trustee Orientation, *Council on Foundations. To order, call Family Foundation Services at 202/467-0407 or e-mail family@cof.org.*

Practices to Help Avoid Conflict

- Develop a clear mission and guidelines and adhere to them.

- Develop term limits and or a rotation schedule to allow for a balanced board.

- Develop an orientation and training schedule for new board members so that everyone starts with an understanding of the foundation's mission and the role of trustees.

- Develop a plan for the "next generation" to become involved in the foundation, along with clear succession policies.

- Bring in an outside facilitator or mediator to work with the board.

Family Dynamics—Out in the Open

Want to talk openly with board members about how family dynamics affect the foundation operations? Start with an anonymous assessment survey to see how everyone views the issue. Questions can be similar to those below:

How strongly do you agree or disagree with the following statements?

- We handle conflict well in this family; arguments rarely interfere with or spoil our interactions with one another.

- We do not have a long history of grudges.

- Individuals are valued in this family for their unique contributions.

- This family picks the best people for each job based on ability.

- Family politics (alliances, branch loyalties, hierarchies) do not get in the way of working together.

- We communicate effectively.

- Even when the tasks are hard, working together is enjoyable.

If some members strongly disagree with one or more of the above statements, pose the question: Would the family benefit from facilitation to improve foundation and family relations?

Some of the above questions are from the Council on Foundations publication The Succession Workbook: Continuity Planning for Family Foundations, *by Gersick, Stone et al., 2000. To order, call 888/239-5221 or visit www.cof.org.*

Dealing With Founder's Syndrome

- **Create a solid transition plan.** What if the founder left? Who would quickly step in? Where are the files and records?

- **Communicate** often and honestly with the founder and with each other.

- **Be willing to ask for and accept help** from one another and, if need be, from an outside facilitator.

- **Conduct regular and realistic strategic planning** with one another.

- **Make decisions based on mission, planning, and affordability**—not on urgent requests from an individual member.

- **Support the founder** with ongoing coaching and affirmation. In time, the founder will change to the extent that he or she feels safe, understands the reasons for change and accepts help along the way.

Dealing with a Disruptive Board Member

If a board member *consistently* disrupts meetings or prevents the organization from working well, it may be appropriate to consider removing the individual from the board. Here are some suggestions:

- Have the board jointly create a code of conduct for member behavior, and consequences (such as removal) for noncompliance.

- Conduct a face-to-face intervention with the person, offering opportunities for open communication and improvement.

- Call in an outside consultant for mediation if necessary.

- Offer a leave of absence.

- Ask the board member to voluntarily resign.

- Remove the board member by a vote.

- Hold an open and confidential discussion with the board after the fact to help air feelings and prepare for the future.

Consensus-Building Strategies

Consensus building refers to the process used to foster dialogue, clarify issues and concerns or make joint decisions among people with diverse viewpoints or expertise. The objectives of consensus building vary widely, from enabling effective collaboration among people working towards a common goal to negotiating recommendations or agreements on highly controversial issues.

Consensus building implies that decisions are made not by majority rule but by the assent of all parties involved. Neutral third parties (mediators, facilitators, arbitrators) can help participants to settle disputes or improve communication in and between meetings or settle disputes.

Whether your family foundation hires an outside third party to assist, the following principles of conflict resolution may help:

- **Create an effective atmosphere.** Establish norms for discussion such as alternating between pro and con arguments or setting time limits.

- **Clarify perceptions.** Successful negotiation or conflict resolution requires a common understanding of a situation and the opposing positions. Do not assume that participants are clear or correct in their perceptions.

- **Focus on individual and shared beliefs.** Members of the board share the goal of working to advance the foundation's mission. If the board starts with that larger shared goal, it may be more likely to find workable solutions.

- **Build shared positive power.** When board members agree to work together as problem solvers rather than as opposing camps, conflicts may be more easily and amicably resolved.

- **Look to the future.** Learn from the past. Conflict is always present on foundation boards; it is a sign that board members are carefully considering each decision. Board members can learn from the process how to be more effective in the future.

- **Generate options.** A solution is more likely to be found if the board generates alternatives.

- **Make mutual-benefit agreements.** Finding solutions that satisfy the primary concerns of the opposing points of view is possible when all parties are willing to make minor concessions.

Excerpted from The Troublesome Board Member, *by Mark Bailey, Board-Source, 1996, www.boardsource.org.*

In Their Own Words:

Group Decisionmaking

One tool that keeps the Klingenstein Third Generation Fund board members engaged is that we have a rule: if someone isn't comfortable with the focus area, we agree not to fund it. For example, at one point, people were split on whether we should fund in areas of race relations. It got contentious and we therefore ended the program. This was hard for me as a staff person since I had put a lot of work into it, but it is important to make decisions as a group. We do not use discretionary grants for this reason.

—*Sally Klingenstein, Klingenstein Third Generation Fund*

COLLEAGUE STORIES:
Grant Proposal Sounding Boards

How do your colleagues build consensus?
The Marcia Brady Tucker Foundation
designed its own version of consensus
building by creating a grant proposal
sounding board. This helped members
improve their grant proposals to the entire
board, thereby avoiding potential tension
that was created by board members who
were ill-prepared to present their proposals.

Like most family foundations, the Marcia
Brady Tucker Foundation faced some conflict among its members. "Certain people
were always bringing grant proposals; others were afraid to do so. Those who did
bring proposals didn't adequately prepare
for questions from the board, leading to
embarrassment and even some family
members dropping out." To avoid that
potential embarrassment, the foundation is
now working on a new process that stream-
lines grantmaking *and* averts negative family dynamics. "The new process involves a
series of checklists and questions that any
given grantmaker would attempt to answer
about a proposal. Proposals first go to a
smaller grants committee who gives the
presenter feedback on how to improve the
request." It is the foundation's hope that
grant proposals will be polished and the
presenter will be well-prepared by the time
his or her request gets to the table. After all,
says Tucker, "families are hard to work
with. We are trying to get away from the
personal hurts and be more businesslike."

A Little Humor Goes a Long Way

A good laugh now and
then—even in the board-
room—can go a long way
toward alleviating tension.
Family foundation boards
are faced with compli-
cated and challenging situations, and a sense of
humor can be a great
asset. Humor can be
used to defuse anxiety
and conflict—a good
laugh can clear the air
and help everyone refo-
cus on the task at hand.
It can also be used to
build rapport among
board members, making
board meetings both
effective *and* fun. Need
some tips for using humor
at meetings? Try including
cartoons in the board
handbooks, or start each
meeting with a playful ice-
breaker. You can find
ideas online at
www.cartoonbank.com
or under keyword
"icebreakers" at
www.meetingwizard.org.

Consultant-Facilitated Retreats

A family foundation retreat is a gathering of members responsible for the governance of a family foundation. The retreat offers an opportunity for members to spend more time together than usual, and it can be a healthy way to deal with family disagreements. Retreats can allow a family or board conflict to be articulated so that the discussion contributes to building consensus.

It is possible to hold a board retreat without the aid of a facilitator. Families who put a very high premium on privacy may choose to conduct their own retreats. A facilitator, however, can bring objectiveness and neutrality to a typically highly charged retreat setting

Consider hiring an outside facilitator to enhance communication among family members. Outside facilitators can bring objectivity and focus to the board, enabling the family to embrace different views and opinions. Bringing in a consultant also relieves a family member from the dual role of advocating a fair process for the foundation members, while advocating for his or her own interests.

Where do you find foundation consultants? This list will give you a start:

- Foundation and nonprofit colleagues
- Council on Foundations Family Foundation Services department (family@cof.org)
- Regional associations of grantmakers (www.givingforum.org)
- Local community foundations (www.communityfoundationlocator.org)
- Journals and trade magazines such as *Foundation News & Commentary* (www.foundationnews.org), *More Than Money* (www.morethanmoney.org), *Family Business Review* (www.ffi.org)
- The web. Sites such as Charity Channel (www.charitychannel.com/consultants) provide a paid, online registry system that helps nonprofits locate consultants.

In Their Own Words:

Helping Consultants Help You

There are a few things that always help me do my job better as a consultant to a family foundation. One thing a board can do—share with me on a confidential basis information about potentially explosive dynamics that may help avoid some difficult situations and help me develop strategies to keep conflicts from occurring in the future. There is no substitute for complete candor, honesty and full disclosure—all of which are held in confidence.

—Anne Morgan, Consultant

TOOL BOX:
Consensus Building and Consultants

Resources on Consensus Building

Conflict Management Group
CMG helps people, divided by conflict, to see new opportunities for managing their differences constructively through peaceful means. For more information, contact: Conflict Management Group, 20 University Road, Cambridge, MA 02138; 617/354-5444; www.cmgroup.org.

Consensus Building Institute
A nonprofit organization providing seminars, training and in the areas of consensus building and dispute resolution. For more information, contact: Consensus Building Institute, 131 Mt. Auburn Street, Cambridge, MA 02138, 617/492-1414; fax: 617/492-1919; www.cbuilding.org.

Program on Negotiation for Senior Executives
Offers a program on mutual gains negotiation techniques that "separates the people from the problem and turn differences into mutual gains." For more information, contact: Center for Management Research, 55 William Street, Suite 210, Wellesley, MA 02181, 781/239-1111; fax: 781/239-1546; www.pon.execseminars.com.

Association for Conflict Resolution
International association of dispute resolution professionals. Produces a variety of publications and reports, convenes conferences and regional meetings. For more information, contact: Association for Conflict Resolution, 1015 18th Street NW, Suite 1150, Washington, DC 20036, 202/464-9700; fax: 202/464-9720; www.acresolution.org.

How to Plan a Retreat with a Facilitator

1. **Identify two or three board members to serve on a planning committee.** A planning committee ensures that the ideas for the retreat come from more than one person and that there is ownership by several people.

2. **Agree on the initial purposes or goals for the retreat.** Be reasonable in your expectations for yourself and for the facilitator. Do not expect to resolve long-held family value conflicts easily or quickly.

3. **Agree on a process for selecting a facilitator and select one.** Selecting a facilitator requires identifying criteria, talking with people in the field to get suggestions, soliciting information on credentials and references from the candidates and conducting interviews.

4. **Create a plan for proceeding with the facilitator.** For instance, will the facilitator interview board members privately and in advance of the retreat or perhaps send out written surveys to the board? How will the facilitator work with the planning committee?

5. **Develop an agenda.** Consider holding a conference call with the planning committee and sending materials to board members in advance.

6. **Determine and communicate the role of staff, if applicable, in a retreat.** In some family foundations, staff help plan the retreat, arrange logistics, sit in on most meetings and prepare follow-up notes and activities. Many families want some time in the retreat without staff to discuss sensitive family or staff issues. If this is the case, the board should explain its reasons for closed-door sessions honestly to the staff.

For more information on family foundation retreats, read the *Family Foundation Retreat Guide*, Council on Foundations, 1995. To order, call 888/239-5221 or visit www.cof.org.

Chapter in Sum: Dealing with Differences

What Success Looks Like

Here are some suggestions for how family foundations can communicate well and avoid conflicts:

- Create a safe environment.
- Listen without judgment.
- Speak respectfully to one another.
- Have a sense of play and humor.
- Respect one another's privacy.
- Explore different interests.
- Work through differences when they arise.
- View all family and board members as *problem solvers*, not as friends or adversaries.
- Be soft on people but hard on problems.
- Label the behavior, not the person.
- Seek outside help for problems you cannot resolve.

Chapter 3:
The Unexpected and Inevitable

In this chapter:

- Death of a Foundation Leader
- Fluctuating Assets
- Board Members Who Don't Meet Their Potential

Life is filled with unexplainable, unexpected and often inevitable occurrences. Sometimes it seems that the only consistency we can count on is change. Some change brings wonderful possibilities: a baby is born, a marriage takes place, a group of people come together for a common philanthropic purpose. Other change creates periods of instability in an otherwise solid sense of being: a loved one becomes ill or dies, a family disperses, an irreconcilable conflict arises. Sudden or significant change can leave one feeling vulnerable, confused and wondering: *What am I here for? What is most important? How can I do better in the world, for the world?*

Change can create an imbalance and anxiety not only within you but also in your relationships with others. It's hard enough dealing with change on a personal level. As a member of a family foundation, you must also negotiate that change on a relationship level and an organizational one. Members must not only respond to the stress on individuals and the family but also on the foundation enterprise.

Death of a Foundation Leader

The death of a foundation leader is likely to be the largest change a family foundation will undergo. Suddenly—or not so suddenly, depending on the person's condition—the family must grapple not only with grief but also with an onslaught of financial, legal and organizational issues. This section provides guidance and information to assist the family and foundation with its decisions when a foundation leader dies, and tools to plan ahead for such a circumstance. For simplicity, this section will interchange the words "foundation leader," "donor," and "founder"; however, the information is the same for any foundation leader, board or staff.

The death of a foundation leader can affect foundation operations in very different ways. On one hand, administrative changes may arise because of a significant increase in assets. On another, there may be philosophical changes in how the foundation is run and who is doing the running.

After a donor dies, relationships between staff and board members may also change, as may their expected roles. Depending on the different leadership styles of the foundation president, the staff may be required to be more hands-on or hands-off than they were previously. While staff may be able to prepare administratively for a change in leadership, it can be harder to prepare for the more subtle personal and behavioral changes.

"Don't you think it's time you started thinking about your legacy?"

In Their Own Words:

Changing Relationships and Roles

Charles and Lynn Schusterman formed their family foundation in 1987, just a few years after Mr. Schusterman had been diagnosed with chronic myelogenic leukemia. They hired the first member of their professional staff in 1994 and, working as a team over the course of the next six years, grew their foundation into one of the largest and most influential Jewish philanthropic efforts in the world.

In December 2000, Charles Schusterman finally succumbed to illnesses and complications that resulted from his 17-year battle against cancer. The succession plan the Schusterman family developed when they created their foundation was implemented immediately. Lynn replaced Charles as president of the foundation and their daughter, Stacy, filled the vice-presidency Lynn had held for more than a decade.

Both on paper and on the surface, the leadership transition went as smoothly as expected. It certainly came as no surprise to anyone that Charles predeceased Lynn, and everyone understood the roles they were expected to play when Charles passed away. Our work continued unabated and, from the perspective of most on the outside, the passing of the torch from Charles to Lynn was largely free from difficulty.

And yet, as prepared as we thought we were for that moment, we soon realized that our simple and straightforward succession plan was woefully inadequate. We learned that a leadership transition, even one that is fully expected and genuinely supported by everyone involved, is a complex and complicated process.

While all of us knew what was supposed to happen when Charles died, we were unprepared for the issues that ultimately surfaced as a result of the manner in which each of us responded to our new reality. What we soon discovered was the extent to which Charles had been much more than our president; he was our center of gravity. He set our agenda, he affected our behaviors and he contained our environment. We quickly realized that he had influenced every aspect of our work and of our relationships with each other, even without being directly involved.

Without Charles acting as a tether, our transition involved much more than a reassignment of roles. It required us to reorient ourselves to each other, to redefine our personal and professional relationships in a world without Charles. We had to learn to adapt to a new style of leadership, to acclimate ourselves to a new culture and to work differently to achieve a new set of expectations.

For example, Lynn is much more involved than Charles used to be in the day-to-day operations of our foundation. She wants to be kept completely up to date on as many issues as possible and communicates on a daily basis with both our program officers and our grants manager. Lynn also travels more often and is otherwise

"How will family members act differently once that leader is gone?"

—Sanford Cardin

more accessible to the public than Charles. Both of these differences have resulted in significant changes in the way each of us on the professional staff at our foundation fulfills our individual and collective responsibilities.

In retrospect, our leadership transition took place over two years and involved two distinct phases. The initial period lasted approximately one year and included what we felt was an appropriate mourning process. Even in death, Charles continued to act as a center of gravity and moderating influence. Our succession plan was implemented without rancor, and everyone contributed to making certain the foundation continued to work hard to fulfill the mission and vision of its founders.

The second phase of the transition also lasted one year. Unlike its predecessor, this period was difficult and challenging. Reorientation and realignment were its hallmarks on every level and in every regard. This was the part of the process for which we were largely unprepared and, had we done a better job thinking through all aspects of changes in leadership before Charles died, was a journey we could have made much more easily.

We share this story with others to help them avoid some of the unnecessary and frustrating experiences we endured before emerging as an even stronger, more cohesive foundation than ever before."

—Sanford R. Cardin, Executive Director, Charles and Lynn Schusterman Family Foundation

In Their Own Words:

Changing Dollars vs. Changing Dynamics

The Dyson Foundation was formed in 1957 by Charles and Margaret Dyson. When Mr. Dyson began having significant health problems, we began planning in advance. We talked to the New York Times months before he died, and we developed a public relations plan—with pre-written press releases and obituaries. While it may have seemed morbid to do this when Mr. Dyson was still alive, we would have been unprepared if we hadn't taken all of these steps. At his death in 1997, the foundation received over $250 million in assets and the grantmaking increased from $2–3 million to $12–13 million per year.

Two years after Mr. Dyson died, his adult daughter, Anne Dyson, developed breast cancer and died within a year, quite unexpectedly. At the time, she was the principal public figure in the foundation. At the time of both deaths, the foundation served as a de facto family office in dealing with the public and the media.

Experiencing the death of both foundation leaders within a short time had greater consequences than we expected, especially related to the increase in assets and public visibility. These two deaths had very different [effects]: Mr. Dyson's death changed total dollars, and Anne Dyson's death changed the dynamics even more profoundly—the foundation's priorities, grantmaking and board membership.

—*Diana Gurieva, Executive Director, The Dyson Foundation*

"People plan for their wealth, but not their death. It is hard enough for the family to manage their emotions at the time of a loved one's death, much less foundation dynamics."

—Diana Gurieva

When a donor dies, often the foundation office becomes a main point of contact for the family and for the public. Staff or current board members can assist with many practical concerns. "When our founder Elmer Rasmuson passed, my role as the foundation's administrator was to be available for the family, to handle the media, and to assist with the obituary and letting people know," says Diane Kaplan of the Rasmuson Foundation.

Another example is the Russell Family Foundation. "After one of our founders, Jane Russell, died, the staff tried to create a healing space where the foundation didn't have to be a distraction to the family," says foundation executive director Richard Woo. "It was a time for us to plan for the future, but foremost a time for them to recover. The staff ran the foundation operations so that the family could take a hiatus. Now that they are coming out of a quiet mode, the board has formed a subgroup to determine the best way to honor Jane's legacy."

Preparing for the Future

Whether the death of a donor is unexpected or the outcome of a long illness, it can still leave loved ones and foundation associates feeling numb and bewildered. At these times, even simple decisions can seem overwhelming. The loss can cause a family and board great grief, complicated by the fact that they must act on affairs and make immediate plans.

In most cases, grief pulls a family together to support each other through the mutual loss. However, grief can push family members away from one another, escalating any underlying tension that may have existed. Preparation can save the family heartache and the foundation time when death does occur.

One way to prepare for the future is by asking the founder to craft a letter of *donor intent*. Donor intent refers to the charitable actions, legacy and values of the original donor of a foundation. Defining and drafting a statement of donor intent can be difficult. Not only must donors determine—and describe—the values they wish to impart through the foundation, but they also must think about whether and how these values will endure in the future, after their deaths. If the donors do not communicate these values while they are living, board members are left with no choice but to infer intent—not an easy task. At times, a board may wonder if they are following the donor's wishes.

For Margaret Riecker, president of the Harry A. and Margaret D. Towsley Foundation, passing on the donor's values to the third and fourth generations proved difficult.

"We had to rely on word of mouth, informal discussions and board retreats to share the donor's interests and intentions for the foundation's giving. I urge all donors to develop an oral history on video or some other method to guide future generations of trustees."

"Your foundation doesn't have to be around for 100 years to start planning ahead."

—Deva Hirsch

COLLEAGUE STORIES:
Videos Help Families
Prepare for the Inevitable

If donors share their intent for the future of the foundation *prior* to their death, the remaining and future board members will have a much easier time carrying that intention forward. One of the best ways to share donor intent is by creating a video—something tangible to which the family can refer for years to come.

When Arthur M. Blank's daughter and foundation staff asked him to consider making a video, he agreed that it would be important. Even though the foundation had only been active for five years, Blank understood the importance of preserving his wishes. The staff of the Blank Foundation developed questions and hired a videographer to film and edit the 20-minute video, which was filmed in Blank's home. Questions touched on governance, perpetuity, grantmaking and the donor's values. The staff unveiled the video at a board retreat and has since distributed it to trustees, family members and other family foundations.

According to co-executive director Deva Hirsch, the video accomplished three goals: (1) to prompt the donor to articulate his own long-term goals and aspirations for the foundation; (2) to give his family members an opportunity to hear him describe his values; and (3) to give the foundation board and staff direction and clarity in carrying out his wishes in the future. "It's uncomfortable thinking about a loved one leaving our lives, but if you don't know their wishes, it would feel even worse," said Hirsch. "We work closely with our founder and trustees now to ensure we understand their goals and wishes for the future. You don't have to be around for 100 years to start planning ahead."

TOOL BOX:
Death of a Foundation Leader

Questions to Think About

- Has the foundation experienced or anticipated the death of a donor or board chair?
- What difficulties did/would you encounter in such a transition?
- In what ways can the foundation prepare in advance?

Preparing for Death in Advance

Following are a few tips to help the family and the foundation prepare:

- Ask the donor to communicate his or her intent for the foundation—be it in a biography, personal memoirs, a letter, a video, and/or talks with the other board and family members.
- Ask the donor to establish a process, such as a joint decision by a board sub-committee, to appoint a successor to lead.
- Review the foundation bylaws to make sure they are in good order.
- Ask the donor to put his or her affairs and paperwork in order.
- Pre-write obituaries.
- Pre-write press releases announcing the death.
- Create a list of who will need to be notified—family, friends, associates, vendors, the public.
- Update media and mailing contact information.
- Prepare to order death announcements.

When a death occurs, the family will usually:

- Review any instructions left by the deceased (regarding funeral and/or burial arrangements).
- Notify employers, attorneys, insurance companies, the Social Security Administration and banks.

- Gather important papers, including the will or trust, estate planning documents, deeds, business agreements, tax returns, bank accounts, safe deposit arrangements, earnings statements, birth and marriage certificates, military discharge papers, Social Security Number, vehicle registration, loan payment books, bills, etc.

- Begin or coordinate the probate process. For more information, visit www.unclefed.com/AuthorsRow/Newland/pass_on.html.

In some cases, the family may ask the foundation board or staff members to assist. If this is the case, foundation members can:

- Make initial telephone calls to family, friends, associates, and clergy.

- Send death announcements.

- Help plan and coordinate memorials.

- Finalize obituaries and press release.

- Help write the eulogy, if appropriate.

How to Write an Obituary

Customs and traditions for writing an obituary notice may vary depending on the family's religious affiliation, and ethnic or regional background. You may find it beneficial to look at an obituary notice in your local newspaper to get a better idea of how they are presented. In some cases, funeral homes can assist with writing obituaries. Obituaries typically include the following:

- Full name, age, date of death and place of death

- List family and any predeceased relatives

- A description of the deceased's leadership in the family foundation: when he or she founded or joined the foundation, the values and mission, the contributions, how the deceased made a difference through the work of the foundation

- Background—former employer(s), military service, memberships, etc.

- Personal accomplishments or passions

- Information regarding visitation times, funeral services, memorials, mass services etc.

- Charities or memorial funds to which people may make donations.

To read samples, see the *Sample Obituary* and *Sample Press Release* on pages 143 and 144.

How to Write a Memorial Document

Some foundations choose to create a memorial document to the deceased donor—be it a biography, a preface to the annual report or simply a family scrapbook. Often it is the board's strong desire to provide an ongoing memorial presence in honor of the dead person or persons as a way of ensuring they are remembered. It takes great strength and concentration to sum up a person's life in a few paragraphs or pages. However, it is a gesture that the family and foundation members will appreciate and remember for generations to come.

Where do you start? The memorial can include information about the person's life and work, but also it can express the feelings and experiences of the person memorializing the life—and loss—of the loved one. Here are a few questions and tips to help guide your writing:

- How did you and the deceased become close?

- Is there a humorous or touching event that represents the essence of the person?

- What was your loved one's greatest contribution to the family, the foundation, the community?

- What did you and others admire about the deceased?

- What will you miss most about him or her?

To read a sample, see the *Sample Memorial Document* on page 145.

Donor Intent Questions

The following questions give you points of reference to begin communicating a donor's intent. These can also serve as prompts for a personal interview, an oral history audiotape or a video:

- Why did you start (or join) the foundation?

- What were the key moments in your life that made you think about helping others?

- When was the first time you volunteered your time or talents?

- Who were the major influences in your life, and how did they influence your philanthropy?

- What did you hope to accomplish through a foundation and has that changed over time?

- What caused your interest in the particular areas that the foundation funds?

- What is the most important value you hope to pass on to your family?

- What do you consider the foundation's biggest success?

- What do you envision for the foundation in the future (board, operations, funding focus)?

- Should the foundation exist in perpetuity?

- How important is it that future generations follow your lead in what you fund?

- If friction occurred in the family because of the foundation, what would you like to see happen?

To read a sample donor intent letter, see the *Sample Letter of Donor Intent* on page 141.

Sites to See

- **www.unclefed.com/AuthorsRow/Newland/pass_on.html.**
  Offers information on the probate process.

- **www.obituariestoday.com.**
  Includes information on how to write obituaries.

- **www.thefuneraldirectory.com.**
  Resources, articles, pre-planning information and more.

Fluctuating Assets

Who would think of a rise in assets as a problem? In fact, many family foundations face the challenge of how to manage a surge in assets. Typically, an increase in funds results from the death of a donor, the sale of a family business or capital gains on investments. Sometimes, it comes from the largesse of a living donor. This growth can leave foundations wondering how they will spend their increased funds and how the staff will manage it. A growth in assets can transform business as usual, affecting everything from a change in office space and staff to a complete revamp of mission and goals.

COLLEAGUE STORIES:
Staffing Up

When a donor dies and leaves a significant amount of his/her estate to the foundation, it changes the way the foundation will be run. In order to have the administrative resources to meet the increased payout obligation, a foundation often must hire or add staff as a first order of business. The Rasmuson Foundation did just this after its founder, Elmer Rasmuson, died in December 2000, increasing the foundation assets from $9 million to $450 million in a slow-rolling movement from his estate. The donor, however, was always one to plan ahead, even for what would happen after his own death. Diane Kaplan was hired in 1995 as grants administrator and worked part time for six years to prepare for the transition. She put systems in place such as grant priorities and guidelines, an application brochure and a website. She also established connections between the board and the larger foundation world. After the foundation leader's death, Kaplan became a full-time employee and hired a full staff of seven in 2001. "Hiring staff brought on new transitions in infrastructure. We had to acquire an office and furnish it, create filing procedures, policies, insurance plans, retirement plans, etc.," said Kaplan. "As we learned from this experience, the transitions occurring after the death of the donor may last for years."

COLLEAGUE STORIES:
Make Big Changes Slowly

An increase in assets brings great opportunity to family foundations and can create what looks like a whole new enterprise—a bigger staff, a different office, new guidelines, more structure. But as other foundations will attest, it can be wise to take time during transitions and to think all the changes through before jumping.

The members of the Gaylord and Dorothy Donnelley Foundation in Chicago underwent a surge in assets in the early 1990s. For nearly a decade, the president administered the foundation's grantmaking single-handedly. After Gaylord Donnelley's death in 1992, the foundation assets jumped from $12 million to $55 million. With the president approaching retirement, the board, consisting of four family members and seven non-family members, took time out to ponder its next steps. Rather than change their mission and guidelines right away, the trustees decided to hold firm to the current grantmaking focus while handling other pressing matters.

Upon hiring an executive director, Judith Stockdale, the foundation hunted for larger offices, developed its computer capacity, updated the accounting system and gradually enlarged the staff. "While it's tempting to rush out new guidelines to quell the clamor for more and bigger grants, it would have been foolhardy for us to make big changes quickly," says Stockdale. Taking one change at a time can be the best way to handle change.

A Time to Revisit the Mission

In spite of the rapid changes that occur when a foundation grows significantly in assets, it should be a time of reflection and renewal. More assets mean more administrative work, which can require additional staff or volunteers. More assets also mean more opportunity to fund organizations and communities never before considered. Many boards will take this opportunity to examine the foundation's current grantmaking program—its mission, guidelines and/or strategies—to make sure it is still relevant to the community and to individual board members. Even if board members decide to continue with their current focus, they may shift how grants are made—for example, funding fewer but larger grants or vice versa. Whatever a board decides, the discussion is an important one to have.

In Their Own Words:

A Mission More Relevant

"My grandparents founded the Albert J. Speh, Jr. and Claire R. Speh Foundation in 1998. We set a broad mission and included the founders and their children on the board. When my grandfather died, the assets went from $3 million to $17 million. Doing work with my grandfather was passionate and important. Losing him made family members realize that this isn't the work that they would necessarily do. It became apparent that board members were reading proposals where they didn't know the areas or communities represented. People began to lose excitement. The atmosphere changed from doing work to honor my grandfather to beginning to understand our personal and shared goals for the foundation. We have now opened up the board to all family members over 18 years of age, which has helped veteran board members become reinvigorated as they look forward to working with their own children and relatives. In addition, we narrowed and re-focused our mission, reinventing the foundation as relevant to Chicago's needs and to the needs of the family."

—*Lynette Malinger, Albert J. Speh, Jr. and Claire R. Speh Foundation*

"When my grandfather died, the climate changed from doing work to honor his passions, to beginning to understand our personal and shared goals for the foundation."

—Lynette Malinger

In Their Own Words:

Change in Assets, Change in Program

My grandfather, the founder of the Sandy River Charitable Foundation, passed away in 1996. It is hard to prepare for someone dying and even harder to prepare for how that will affect foundation operations. Although the foundation did not make any grants before my grandfather passed away, the transfer of assets was a big transition, considering it took place within six months. This changed everything.

The foundation decided to focus significantly on international grantmaking. In order to bring the philanthropy closer to home, however, we developed an "In Your Backyard" program for board members. Since board members live in different areas and have different interests, this program keeps them engaged. We allow a broad range of issues, look for relatively modest grant sizes and look for opportunities that will have a sustaining impact given a determinable grant period. As a requirement, board members have to be involved in the legwork to invite the grant proposal, and the entire board must discuss and vote on each project.

The increase in assets caused the "In Your Backyard" funds to jump significantly and led to larger grants to our national funding program. It allowed the foundation to ramp up grantmaking quickly and efficiently without the sense that we were just throwing money at charitable causes.

—Nathanael Berry, Program Director,
Sandy River Charitable Foundation

TOOL BOX:
Fluctuating Assets

Questions to Think About

- If a donor or family member plans to bequeath substantial assets to the foundation upon death, has the foundation considered the implications on staffing, management and grantmaking?

- How will we meet our increased payout?

- How will the work get done? Does staff need to be added? What are our other options?

- How will this change our grantmaking?

- If applicable, how will the foundation continue its plans to spend down?

- If assets decline dramatically, how will we cut costs?

- If we must change our grantmaking as a result of decreased assets, how will we communicate this to our grantees?

Making Payout

Each year, a private foundation must distribute an amount equal to approximately 5 percent of the average fair market value of its assets for charitable purposes. This rule ensures that foundations cannot be used to accumulate assets unreasonably. A private foundation has 12 months after completing its tax year to make up any shortfall in distribution. Failure to comply with this minimum payout (also called minimum distribution) requirement can result in an initial penalty tax of 15 percent of the foundation's undistributed income.

For more information on what counts toward the payout requirement, read *Family Foundations and the Law*, Council on Foundations, 2002, 888/239-5221 or www.cof.org.

Anticipating a Large Gift?

The Council on Foundations *2003 Foundation Management Survey* asked its family foundation members how many of them anticipated receiving a substantial gift in the next ten years. Thirty-six percent of the respondents anticipated such a gift.

How to Figure Out Payout: Sample Calculation

Example: For the 2003 tax year, Foundation X has a 12-month average fair market value of net total endowment equal to $1 million. During 2003, it paid excise tax payments on its investment income of $1,000. The distributable amount for Foundation X is calculated as follows:

Asset Value		$1,000,000
Cash Held for Charitable Purposes (deduct 1.5 percent)*-	–	15,000
		985,000
Multiply by 5 percent	x	.05
		49,250
Credit for excise tax paid	–	1,000
Distributable Amount	=	**48,250**

*The law presumes that any foundation needs to have cash on hand to conduct business; thus a 1.5% deduction may be taken in asset value.

—Excerpt from *Family Foundations and the Law,*
Council on Foundations, 2002.

How Will the Work Get Done?

Consider Hiring Staff

When a donor dies or assets rise, staff can improve the efficiency and quality of foundation operations through the transition and beyond. Many foundations find that the financial investment in staff salaries pays off. Whether your board is considering hiring its first executive director or administrator or adding program and support staff to an already full office, consider these tools to help you through the process:

■ Create a thorough job description for the position, giving a brief history of the foundation, the position responsibilities, professional and personal qualities desired and application requirements.

■ Use the Council on Foundations *Grantmakers Salary and Benefits Report* or other local and regional surveys to help determine appropriate salary and benefit ranges for new staff positions.

■ Draft a letter stating terms of employment and all expectations and policies.

■ Prepare and conduct regular performance evaluations to aid staff development and determine salary increases.

During Economic Downturns: Ways to Save

A rise in assets may not be the only change a foundation undergoes. With a downturn in the economy, foundations lose assets and look for cost-saving methods. Smaller foundations—those that are board-managed or have one or two staff people—may not have the option of downsizing staff and must turn to other ways to save.

Here are some cost-saving tools that your foundation might consider in times of hardship:

■ **Share space and/or staff** with other foundations, family businesses or nonprofits. Foundations find that sharing resources can significantly reduce administrative costs for all parties involved.

■ **Control printing and advertising costs.** Many foundations are sending letters as their annual reports or making them available online to save printing costs.

■ **Manage on-site expenses** such as compensation and reimbursement for board meeting attendance. Foundations with geographically dispersed members may try alternating teleconferencing with in-person board meetings.

- **Consider use of a "common grant application,"** which can be found through regional associations of grantmakers (www.givingforum.org) or community foundations (www.communityfoundationlocator.org). Standardized grant applications or online applications can streamline the grant request process for both foundation and grantee.

- **Aim for less paperwork.** Consider whether repeat grantees should be required to submit the same paperwork as new grantees. If you've already investigated and determined they are worthy of your support, save your time and theirs by requiring a full-blown application only every few years.

- **Use a peer network.** Team up with other like-minded foundations to fund or evaluate an organization.

- **Communicate your intentions** with your grantees and your community. If they are aware of why you are taking necessary cost-saving steps, they will be willing to work with you to produce a "win–win" outcome for all parties involved.

Board Members Who Don't Meet Their Potential

It can become a difficult situation when board members, for a variety of reasons, become unable to perform their duties. For example, an individual may become ill or incapacitated. Perhaps the person becomes too elderly to physically attend the meetings or may suffer from dementia. A board member might deal with alcohol or drug abuse, or in extreme scenarios, may commit a criminal offense. In a foundation setting, these personal challenges affect both the individual and the board as a whole.

Aside from illness, age and other, more unusual circumstances, a common scenario is that board members don't have time outside of their careers or personal lives to meet their board responsibilities. Boards should encourage members to be open and honest in this situation, instead of taking on more than they can handle. This is how the Sandy River Charitable Foundation faces the situation, for example. According to program director Nathanael Berry, "We recognize that family members lead full and complicated lives. There is no stigma attached to admitting one has simply too much to do."

In all of the above cases, there will be times when board members may want to retire from their responsibilities while they tend to personal issues. Although it may be slightly uncomfortable, this may be the best solution for everyone involved. If individuals want to remain on the board even though they aren't meeting their potential as a board member, it may result in an unfortunate effect on a foundation's performance and other board members' morale.

What can boards do in such a case? The first step is to make clear the foundation's expectations for all members. Below are two lists: the ten basic qualities of a good board member and a list of what foundation boards do. You might copy these lists for board members or use this list as a baseline for developing your board's own list of expectations.

Ten Basic Qualities of a Good Board Member

1. Interest in and concern for the foundation and its field(s) of interest

2. For the special-purpose foundation, some understanding of the specific area of interest, and for the general-purpose foundation, some broad perspective on the problems of society

3. Objectivity and impartiality

4. Special skills, for example, management, investment experience, familiarity with budgets, knowledge of the law

5. Capacity for teamwork and for arriving at and accepting group decisions

6. Willingness to work

7. Practical wisdom

8. Commitment to the foundation as a whole and not to special interests or constituencies

9. Commitment to the idea of philanthropic foundations

10. Moral sensitivity to the act of and the need for giving.

From Foundation Trusteeship: Service in the Public Interest, *by John W. Nason for the Council on Foundations, The Foundation Center, 1989, page 56.*

What Does a Foundation Board Do?

As part of its many roles and responsibilities, a foundation board:

- Adheres to the regulations that govern foundations

- Maintains fiduciary stewardship and accountability

- Defines and periodically reviews the values, vision and mission statements of the foundation

- Creates bylaws describing how the foundation will be governed

- Recruits and orients other board members; defines member roles and responsibilities

- Sets policy on investments, spending, hiring, personnel, and compensation

- Hires, supports and evaluates the executive director/foundation manager

- Ensures strategic planning for the foundation

- Determines grant goals and grant guidelines

- Makes funding decisions; monitors and evaluates programs

- Assesses its work as a board and as a foundation

- Communicates its work to the public.

In Their Own Words:

Defining Expectations

"If family foundations don't define the jobs that people will handle, it can cause internal conflict—just as it would with any organization. In order to make sure goals and expectations are met, it is especially important to define jobs and complete performance evaluations of board and staff members. By doing this, family foundations can maintain objectivity in a very subjective—and personal—environment."

—Ann Ostergaard, Personnel Consultant

The Alcoholic Board Member: A Hypothetical Scenario

The Treasurer of the XYZ Family Foundation developed an addiction to alcohol. Ms. A only drank moderately in public and at family gatherings, so the board did not detect her addiction at first. They were puzzled, however, by her rapid and dramatic mood swings. She sometimes raved and ranted, other times withdrew sadly, and would appear pleasant and professional in between. At board meetings, Ms. A seemed either meddlesome and impatient or completely absent-minded for serious business.

Alcohol or drug addiction is sometimes hard to recognize. Whether the board knows explicitly about the abuse or not, they do know that Ms. A's behavior is affecting the foundation performance. Simple term limits or other preventive strategies could ward off this continuing problem, saving the board's sanity and hopefully giving Ms. A time off to get the help she needs.

Create Preventive Policies

Creating policies in the following areas will help the board take action in events where a board member cannot meet his or her responsibilities:

- Board member job descriptions
- Performance appraisals
- Term limits
- Committee or advisory group service
- Leaves of absence
- Board removal.

TOOL BOX:
Board Members Who Don't Meet Their Potential

Questions to Think About

■ Has the board ever considered how to remove someone because of physi-
cal/mental illness, substance abuse, family estrangement, criminal behavior
or other reason?

■ How did/would you accomplish this?

■ If you did, what was the impact? What would the board do differently?

Board Member Job Descriptions

A small but growing number of foundations develop job descriptions for their board
members. Approximately 14 percent of family foundations said they have a written
position description for at least one of their board members, well below the overall
average of 26 percent for all foundation types.* Job descriptions help board members understand their roles and responsibilities, and clarify the relationships
between the board and staff (if present). They also serve as a tool for members to
evaluate their own performance or evaluate their peers.

A job description can take any format. Most are one or two pages and include the
function, duties and desired characteristics of a board member. When drafting a
job description, remember that the responsibilities of the overall board are different from those of its individual members. Job descriptions outline expectations
and can be used to show when they are not being met.

For a sample job description, see *Sample Board Member Job Descriptions*, pages
136 and 137.
*From *Foundation Management Series, 10th edition, Volume 2: Governing Boards*,
Council on Foundations, 2002, p.10.

Performance Appraisals

Regular performance self-appraisals can be a useful and less formal tool in improving overall board performance, operations and outreach. Setting predetermined
criteria as a group also provides an objective way to remove inactive, ineffective or
counterproductive members. Ask board members to evaluate their own individual
performance. Some boards use a simple and confidential survey format, asking
people to rate themselves in different areas on a scale of one to five. The same
format can be used for peer reviews, using a one-page list of board members. On
any survey, it helps to include open-ended questions to get a variety of responses.

Start by evaluating the board as a group. Ask yourselves the following questions:

- Are we structured well?

- Is our role clear?

- What can we do to improve the board?

For sample board member evaluations, see the *Sample Board Member Self-Evaluation*, page 138.

Term Limits

Many boards establish not only board terms, but also term limits, such as two-year terms with a limit of three consecutive terms. In such a situation, for example, a board member cannot serve more than six consecutive years without a "break" from the board. After a year or two off the board, an individual might once again be eligible for election to the board. In addition to creating opportunities for new blood on the board, proponents feel that term limits also provide a non-confrontational way to ease ineffective board members off the board.

For sample term limit policies, see the *Sample Term Limit and Rotation Policy* on page 132 or contact the Council on Foundations at family@cof.org.

Committees or Advisory Groups

Committees may be the answer for family members who, for a number of personal reasons, can't meet full board duties. Committees, or smaller advisory groups, offer a service to the board while limiting the responsibilities and time requirements of members.

Many boards have at least two standing committees—governance and finance. The governance committee is responsible for recruiting, orienting, and educating new members, a process that continues year-round. The finance committee makes sure that the foundation's resources are being managed adequately. A foundation board would likely have an investment committee as well.

Task forces are groups that meet around a particular issue that has a beginning and an end. Planning a board retreat, reviewing bylaws or investigating a new program area are examples of projects that would be better suited to a task force than a standing committee. If, at the end of the task force's work, the board discovers that the issue has become an ongoing one, the board can always form a committee on that issue.

Leaves of Absence

Boards may wish to make it possible for individuals to take a leave of absence if they have health problems, work issues, or other reasons why they cannot participate fully during the current term. A board member can maintain formal membership (but not, for example, be included for purposes of determining a quorum) if he or she is "on disability leave" or "taking six months' leave." Suggesting a leave of absence to a board member who is, for example, failing to do tasks he or she agreed to do, offers a gracious exit and allows the board to assign tasks elsewhere.

Board Removal

If a board member has failed to attend several meetings in a row or has become an impediment to the board's work, the board president can meet informally with the board member in question. In person or on the telephone, the board president can negotiate a plan with the person or request a resignation. With proper board leadership, board members who are not meeting their responsibilities can be guided toward either improving their behavior or quietly resigning.

Occasionally, a family foundation board will have the difficult task of removing a board member. This can be awkward for a number of reasons, especially if a board member suffers an unforeseen illness, disability or abuse problem. The person might believe that he or she can still perform or deny that there is a problem. Even if the board member's intentions are good, their behavior or situation may obstruct the rest of the board from functioning effectively.

Although the need for such a provision is rare, foundations should provide terms for removing a board member in their bylaws. Having pre-written policies can make it easier for the board to handle a difficult situation in the most objective way possible. It can also help assuage personal tension or hurt feelings at the time of removal, allowing the board to point at the policy instead of the person.

Chapter in Sum: The Unexplained and Inevitable

What Success Looks Like

What are some indications that a foundation has successfully prepared for death or illness of a donor, asset change or crisis?

- The donor has participated in planning what will follow his or her death.
- There is a plan for leadership transition, and possibly a pre-selected successor.
- The foundation celebrates the legacy created by its donor.
- There are bylaws covering terms, rotation and board member removal.
- The foundation has the ability, resources and space to house staff if needed.
- There are solid investment and spending policies in place, and expert advice is sought when revisiting them.
- There are tools to guide performance, such as job descriptions, performance objectives and evaluations.
- The foundation has connections within the field for learning and support.

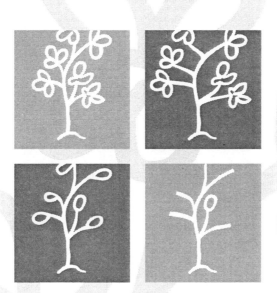

Part 2

Solutions

Grantmaking Alternatives

In Times of Change, Revisit the Mission

If it appears that the purpose of the grantmaking has become dated and no longer speaks to what the board feels is an essential need, the board may be able to adopt a new mission. The board's authority in this regard depends on whether the founder imposed legal restrictions on the foundation's activities that the board must continue to observe and, to some extent, on the foundation's organizational structure—usually it is easier to change the purposes of a charitable corporation than those of a charitable trust. Consult an attorney if there is any doubt about the board's power to change the foundation's purposes. If you do decide to revise the mission, consider the following tips:

- Hold a facilitated family retreat to discuss board members' ideologies, interests and geography.
- Call upon the expertise and insight of individuals beyond the family, board and staff.
- Research funding gaps in your community or focus area.
- Seek advice and assistance from grantmaking professionals at other private foundations.

COLLEAGUE STORIES:
Flexibility in The Randall L. Tobias Foundation

Sometimes transitions can cause tension between the foundation and grantees.

The Randall L. Tobias Foundation recently transitioned from reactive grantmaking to a board-initiated funding style. The Tobias Foundation, created in 1994 to inspire excellence in education, received grant requests twice yearly from nonprofit organizations and school systems seeking funds for inspired educational programming. The application process was designed to be grant-seeker friendly, with a relatively concise proposal form and readily available assistance from foundation staff. In the three years of reactive grant making, the Tobias Foundation provided over $1.5 million to worthy recipients that met the funding criteria.

Randall Tobias and his two children, Paige T. Button and Todd C. Tobias, constitute the board of directors of the foundation. They began to question the value of the process-driven funding they were overseeing and created some unique "grants" of their own—such as a holiday gift to support the education of each child from their former New Jersey hometown who lost a parent in the September 11, 2001 attacks. With the direction of some of Indiana's most capable educators, the Tobiases announced the development of a statewide literacy initiative, designed to inspire excellence in the teaching of reading and writing. The family has dedicated more than $750,000 to this three-year Literacy for Life program that may well serve as a model for the teaching of reading throughout the state.

The Tobias Foundation's board of directors concluded that for this time in their lives, the board-initiated funding better suited their charitable intentions. With a budget the size of their prior grant making expenditures, they actively engaged themselves in the development of well-researched programs that received more concentrated resources and attention. The family members were gratified and the foundation initiatives thrived.

Just as the foundation's grant process had been very deliberately announced four years earlier, it was imperative that the change in funding procedures be announced just as deliberately. The Tobias Foundation grantees received personal letters, followed by a mailing to fellow funders and press releases directed to the community at large. The news was a disappointment to the nonprofit sector that had appreciated the foundation's transparency and enthusiastic support of inspired learning in the community. However, they appreciated the Tobias family's continued generosity and understood that funding strategies may evolve, especially when dealing with a living donor.

Discretionary Programs

Discretionary grants are funds distributed at the discretion of one or more board members or, in some cases, principal staff persons. Many foundations offer discretionary grants to allow board members or staff to support organizations that the foundation may not traditionally fund. Aside from affecting a wider range of issues or geography, the discretionary fund serves to acknowledge board members for their volunteer service and enables them to support charities for which they have individual concern. With this small vehicle to voice personal funding interests, board members can keep the bulk of the foundation's grantmaking dollars on mission. Staff members frequently use their discretionary grants to respond to emergencies or opportunities that must be funded between grant cycles.

These grants do not necessarily require prior approval by the full board of directors, although the board still holds full fiduciary responsibility over all grants made. Some board members may think of discretionary grants as a display of their individual interests and passions. While this may be the case, foundation funds are a public trust and should always be used with the welfare of the community firmly in mind.

Discretionary grants enable different family members, branches or generations to continue the foundation's work while funding in an area of their particular interest.

What's different about discretionary grants?

- Board members are given the right to direct grants, which are often approved after the fact by the full board (assuming they are legal and meet any requirements set by the board).
- There is a set maximum amount.
- They typically involve little board discussion.

According to a recent Council on Foundations survey, nearly half of all family foundations allow board members to make discretionary grants. This is almost twice the overall average of 26 percent for all foundation types. The median maximum amount allowed to board chairs was $10,000, with a range of $200 to $1 million. The median maximum allowed other board members was also $10,000, with a range of $500 to $400,000.

Some balk at the use of discretionary grants, arguing that they are a way to avoid the work it takes to come to consensus on a defined grantmaking focus. They say that funding individual concerns should be done on an individual basis—not as a part of the foundation. Discretionary grants place decisionmaking in the hands of individuals or family branches, as opposed to the family as a whole. For a family hoping to keep the foundation together in perpetuity, excessive reliance on discretionary grants can release tension in the short term, but may fragment involvement over the long term.

Discretionary Grants: Pros and Cons

Discretionary grants can serve to:

- Accommodate differences in values, geography, interests or expertise
- Increase board members' interest, thereby increasing involvement
- Reward board members' participation
- Allocate grantmaking across family branches
- Introduce the next generation to philanthropy
- Incubate new program areas
- Fund outside of mission, or fund an emergency.

On the other hand, they may:

- Thwart grantmaking effectiveness by scattering focus, direction and dollars
- Enable families to avoid working through differences of opinion about good grants and effective philanthropy
- Create a focus on individual or branch decisionmaking, eventually resulting in a foundation splitting or dissolving.

In Their Own Words:

How Family Foundations Use Discretionary Grants

At the Posner-Wallace Foundation, we have developed an escape valve in our foundation. All generations have resisted giving individuals or generations a different degree of influence over parts of the budget. However, we have a rule that anyone can request an unlimited number of checks up to $200 each for 501(c)(3) organizations (or equivalent organizations outside the U.S.) that they are interested in—no questions asked, no debate or approval needed from anyone else. Our reasoning is that an additional ten, 20 or 30 small checks a year do not make a meaningful dent in an overall budget. Moreover, it encourages us to keep our discussions focused on the larger projects and multi-year commitments. It also gives a chance to watch new organizations before developing a bigger financial commitment to them.

—*Jim Posner, Posner-Wallace Foundation*

At the Albert J. Speh, Jr. and Claire R. Speh Foundation, the board members wanted to take a piece of the foundation home with them. The foundation offers some discretionary grants for the second generation: the members of the executive board each receive between $10,000 and $20,000. There are no mission or geographic requirements for where they must grant these funds. The only requirement is that they must involve their family in the philanthropy."

—*Lynette Malinger, Albert J. Speh, Jr. and Claire R. Speh Foundation*

At the Oppenheimer Brothers Foundation, board members budget for primary grants as well as discretionary grants. The foundation has a focused mission, so everyone can still decide together on the primary grants, but can make their own decisions on how to spend the discretionary. The next generation receives up to $1,000 in discretionary grants to spend outside of the foundation's mission.

However, in order to access this money, they must give twenty hours of community service and write about their experience. It is a great learning tool to help them get their feet wet in philanthropy.

—*Tracy Boldemann-Tatkin, Oppenheimer Brothers Foundation*

At the Dyson Foundation, each nonfamily director is allowed to designate $50,000 to organizations in funding areas of their choice. This lets them direct money to issues they care about that may fall outside of the foundation's guidelines. It allows them to focus on the foundation's causes more and rewards them in light of the fact that we don't pay board fees.

—*Diana Gurieva, Dyson Foundation*

The Downside to Discretionary Grants

Discretionary grants are all too often a release valve for pressure. When relied on too heavily, there is little commonality in what family members fund, and then what is the point in doing the philanthropy together? Discretionary grants are a stopgap solution—people periodically should get together to see what the current board and family are invested in. Discretionary grants may lessen the family friction, but if they become too large a percentage of the foundation's grants, they also will undermine the fabric of the mission, making it more likely that the foundation members will have nothing in common in the next generation.

—*Karen Green, Managing Director,*
Family Foundation Services, Council on Foundations

Alternatives to Discretionary Grants

Does the family need additional tools aside from the foundation to meet its philanthropic needs? Perhaps the family hopes to give outside the foundation's mission or to offer an opportunity for the younger generation to gain experience with philanthropy. The foundation might wish to make smaller gifts than is typical of a foundation grant or settle differences in interest or ideology among family members. Discretionary grants can be effective tools in these cases, but there are alternatives.

Before creating a discretionary grants program, board members should also consider vehicles outside of the foundation. Some of these vehicles include:

- Writing personal checks
- Establishing a donor-advised fund at community or other public foundations
- Setting up a supporting organization to a favored charitable organization.

Using funds other than the foundation's, these three options will accomplish what discretionary grants do, while keeping foundation funds (and board members) on mission.

TOOL BOX:
Discretionary Programs

Questions to Think About

If your board decides a discretionary grants program is right for your foundation, the following questions will help your board develop a policy.

- What requirements must board members meet in order to have access to discretionary funds?

- What parameters must discretionary grants meet? Will they be made within or outside of mission? Must they be made within a certain geographical area? Are there additional requirements?

- Who will oversee the discretionary grants to make sure the legal requirements are met? Who will handle the paperwork?

- How can we make sure our mission and guidelines are clear to grantees and the public, so that the discretionary grants don't lead to confusion?

- How can we keep the board members interested in the primary focus of the foundation rather than only their own interests?

- How will we decide which family members are given the right to make discretionary grants, especially if the family grows with generations?

- If we use discretionary grants, how will we make sure the foundation remains effective?

- How can we make sure the discretionary grants budget doesn't escalate from year to year?

Tips for Good Discretionary Grantmaking

- Create a discretionary grants policy (see above). Review it often.

- Create guidelines for discretionary grants.

- Establish a maximum amount that individuals may distribute each year and that the board and staff combined may distribute each year. Make sure it is no more than 10 to 20 percent of the total grantmaking.

- Have board members report occasionally on the discretionary grants they have made. This will help them be accountable and educate other board members on their interests.

- List discretionary grants separately in an annual report or on your web site.

Structural Alternatives

Some foundations are established with a finite life. They make grants of both principal and interest to a particular program or geographic area, usually over a specific period of time, until all of their assets have been spent. Other foundations are established in perpetuity and later decide, for a number of reasons, to close their doors. The foundation's donor or board may decide that it has completed its mission and should therefore terminate. Perhaps there is no next generation of board members to take over. Or maybe the family has grown too large to maintain unity in its interests and ideologies.

When planning to change a foundation's structure, family foundations have many options. They may elect to spend themselves out of business, to transfer their assets to a community foundation, or to continue not as a family foundation, but as an independent foundation with all or a majority of nonfamily members committed to the founding mission. Others may decide to divide the foundation assets into equal parts among family branches or individual family members, or keep the foundation whole but with separate designated funds. Still others decide to merge with another private foundation or become a supporting organization at a favorite charity. And after weighing all the options for terminating, some foundations' boards decide to remain the same unified foundation they always were.

> *"Philanthropic enterprises should come to an end with the close of the philanthropist's life or, at most, a single generation after his death."*
>
> —Julius Rosenwald,
> Sears, Roebuck &
> Company, 1929

For family members looking to restructure, there are a number of viable options for transitioning the foundation into a new form. This chapter discusses options for changing a foundation's structure and the advantages and limitations of each. It offers lessons learned from foundation colleagues who have gone through the process of merging, splitting and terminating. Any family foundation considering these options should seek the assistance of expert legal counsel. Changing the structure of a private foundation is not a do-it-yourself project.

Becoming an Independent Foundation

The size of the foundation often determines how a board will restructure. In general, the larger the corpus, the more likely a foundation will evolve into an independent foundation. Though family may no longer wish to be involved, the endowment may be too large to spend down or fold into another entity.

Some family foundations become independent because the founder has no children and bequeaths the foundation's leadership to selected friends and acquaintances.

The evolution from family to independent foundation is a relatively natural occurrence if the family has already added nonfamily members to the board. Family members will have become accustomed to "outside experts" having a voice in decisionmaking, and they may be more open to replacing their own leadership with new board members.

Merging with Another Foundation

Merging assets and interests with another foundation may be the best way to preserve a foundation over time. Foundations may merge for a number of reasons, some of which include:

- To create one stronger, larger entity with greater assets, rather than two smaller foundations
- To reduce administrative costs by sharing staff, space and resources
- To continue a foundation when there is no one to take over operations.

See also page 11.

Splitting the Foundation

Another way to change the foundation structure is by splitting. Splitting essentially means dividing the foundation assets to create two or more smaller private foundations. In these cases, family branches, generations or other groups take portions of the foundation assets to endow their own separate foundations, with their own grantmaking interests.

There are complex legal rules governing foundation mergers and splits, and foundations should always consult with an attorney before entering into any contract. Revenue Ruling 2002-28, which addresses three common private foundation termination scenarios—divorce, merger and conversion from trust to corporation. For a copy of this ruling, contact the Council on Foundations Legal Services department at legal@cof.org.

COLLEAGUE STORIES:
Parting Ways

The Kerr family was separated by geography and interests. Family members debated whether to keep the $80 million Oklahoma foundation as one endowment with four distinct funding areas or to divide it into separate entities. In the end, the family opted to divide it into four separate foundations.

Breene Kerr, chair of the Grayce B. Kerr Fund in Easton, Maryland says, "Legally it was more difficult to separate into four foundations, and we did lose some economy of scale by having smaller endowments. However, in the long run it is easier for each branch of the family to manage a separate foundation." Kerr believes that the more people are involved in decision-making, the less focused these decisions are. Splitting the foundation has allowed the trustees to focus on grantmaking and spend less time on policy decisions. It has also provided opportunities for more family members to participate.

In 1993, Helen Hunt created a separate grantmaking entity for the work she had previously been doing with her sister Swanee through the Hunt Alternatives Fund. She named it The Sister Fund as a tribute to both Swanee and their sister June, whose shared passion for philanthropy was truly a family affair. Supported by goodwill and launched with a clear sense of purpose and mission, The Sister Fund nonetheless had to tackle issues faced by many foundations that are born of a previously existing entity, as the result of a merger, split-off or conversion.

The Hunt sisters had always acknowledged and respected their different interests and with foresight had established separate endowments even before their formal split six years ago. "They recognized early on that they were doing different work in Denver and New York and set up their endowments to support that," said Kimberly Otis, former executive director of The Sister Fund. "It made for a happy transition and restructuring of a family foundation."

The Sister Fund's story is not unique in the funding world. As old entities give rise to new ones, missions may shift and boards face a fresh set of challenges. Unlike a foundation that is being launched for the first time, these new foundations are often in a position to move to a new level of refinement, to decide what of the past they want to keep and what they want to leave behind. Moving ahead, however, often requires making complex decisions about goals, boards of directors and relationships with constituent communities.

—*Excerpt from "Rebuilding on a Firm Foundation," by Betty Marton,*
    NYRAG Times, *Winter 1998/99, www.nyrag.org.*

COLLEAGUE STORIES:
Splitting—Again and Again

Sometimes, tension about differences is resolved by splitting the assets into more than one foundation. A family foundation that began quite sizably may end up quite small after a series of splits. Splitting may be the best solution in certain circumstances.

Carol Adler's grandparents started a foundation in the 1920s, which was subsequently divided into four after being passed along to their children in the late 1940s. Carol's father's portion, the Cyrus Max Adler Fund, passed at his death in 1959 to Carol and her sisters. "We realized we hadn't been well-schooled on how to run the foundation, and we didn't agree on a lot of things. It was easier to divvy it up." The sisters split the Cyrus Max Adler Fund into three, at which time Carol established the Carol Adler Foundation. In the late 1970s, Carol reorganized the entity to focus on the arts—particularly music, and renamed the foundation The Adler Fund. In addition to the usual grants, it was able to contribute directly to musicians to further their careers. "I never could have done that as one of four co-trustees!" says Carol, who sees the benefits of splitting. "Now I don't have to get permission from other family members as to what I want to do with the fund." Yet Carol knows how small a foundation can become after a series of splits. "I must have the smallest foundation in the world," she says, referring to her $250,000 fund. With such a small foundation in a down economy, Carol recognizes that splitting is an expensive endeavor. What was once one foundation is now four, each with its own administrative expenses such as annual tax filings.

COLLEAGUE STORIES:
Is Splitting the Best Option?

In 2002, the Marcia Brady Tucker Foundation considered splitting among its family branches. The board faced issues of family politics and divergent interests. Moreover, the fourth generation was coming of age and feeling left out.

After the last member of the second generation died, the family took some time to regroup. They hired consultants to facilitate retreats on two separate issues: (1) how to work together with different internal strengths, weaknesses and personality traits; and (2) how to move forward with grantmaking in an organized way. "Through these meetings, we learned that the majority of the people wanted to stay together in spite of the problems we had," says president Luther Tucker, Jr. "They liked having that extended relationship, and didn't want to lose that family feeling."

These retreats helped the family decide to stay together as one foundation. According to Tucker, "We decided that the assets weren't large enough to split and still be effective. Moreover, splitting would only increase the administrative and accounting work and expense."

At the consultants' suggestion, the board changed the bylaws, creating a more structured system with a nominating committee, three-year term limits, a rotation of members and a ratio of board members by generation. "We brought on more fourth-generation members, even appointing some of them as committee heads. They now feel they have more of a voice," says Tucker. The foundation also incorporated a 1:1 matching program, allowing $20,000 per year per board member. "It has been quite an evolution. We've transformed ourselves although we are still in transition."

In Their Own Words:

Solutions Other than Splitting

There are five family branches associated with the Norman Foundation—each has its own small family foundation to give members personal control, and each participates in the Norman Foundation for collective giving. Five years ago, the third generation talked about closing the foundation. The family lost some interest in working together, and there were disagreements about which way to go. It wasn't an easy transition. There was a lot of grumbling and a lot of talk about stopping the foundation altogether.

Instead of splitting the Norman Foundation, however, our family came to a different solution. Some of the assets from the large foundation were carved off to make each of the five family foundations larger (although two family members left their shares in the large foundation).

The Norman Foundation offers board members the opportunity to make donor-advised grants for their personal interests, yet promotes collective decisionmaking on the main fund. The only people either participating in the communal foundation and/or giving donor advised funds are the 16 members of my generation. Some have opted out of the communal foundation altogether; some have left all their funds in the big foundation and some have left a minimum of 51 percent of their funds in the larger foundation and are giving some of their share in donor-advised grants. The minimum donor-advised grant is $1,000. The number of dollars free for the members to give away as donor-advised funds varies from year to year with fluctuations in the value of the foundation and with each member's decision as to what percent of their share they want to leave in the communal foundation.

What advice would I give to others? Over generations with family foundations, the cohesiveness of a large family disperses; everyone has different ideas. People's own concerns have to be met. Otherwise, there will be endless fighting. In the fourth generation, there were 16 of us (as opposed to five in the previous generation). We had to somehow allow for all those individual differences. If people in a family foundation don't agree with the program or want to do something different, you have to allow for that. After all, they are your family—you can't just kick them *out*.

—*Honor Lassalle, President, The Norman Foundation*

Transferring to a Community Foundation or Other Public Charity

Because community foundations have grown in number and strength, some family foundations have chosen them as their means to remain charitably active while relieving board members of the administrative work. Turning assets over to a community foundation or other public charity is by far the easiest method of termination. There are several ways to accomplish this, but the easiest is that the foundation simply distributes its assets to one or more qualifying public charities that have been in existence for at least five years prior to the date of transfer. Most public charities are eligible to receive these distributions.

A foundation that is terminating by transfer to a public charity must observe one other important rule; it may not impose a material restriction or condition on the recipient charity's use of the funds. This does not bar all restrictions. For example, a terminating foundation may limit use of the transferred fund to a specific charitable purpose, such as cancer research, or it may require appropriate acknowledgment of the gift, such as by naming a fund after the family. Making sure that the recipient's governing body is independent of the terminating foundation, and that the recipient gains complete ownership and control of both the transferred assets and the income they produce, is critical to avoiding having restrictions characterized as material.

When transferring to a community foundation, family members may specify in advance that their gift be used only for specific purposes or for the benefit of a specific charity. If the community foundation accepts the gift, it will be bound by this restriction unless changes in circumstances make it impossible to carry out, or the restriction becomes inconsistent with community needs. Once a gift is made, community foundations should welcome, and take seriously, the family's advice concerning potential grants—donors are often an excellent source of information about community need. However, final decisions will be up to the community foundation's board.

For more information, contact the Council's Community Foundation Services department at 202/466-6512, or contact a community foundation in your area. To help you locate the community foundation nearest you, visit www.communityfoundationlocator.org.

Reasons to Roll Over into a Community Foundation

- Lack of family members to carry out the charitable tradition
- Costs associated with running a family foundation
- Lack of desire to handle the foundation's administrative duties
- Desire for the grant support to remain in the community where the money was made, despite the relocation of the family
- Support for a community foundation's growth.

COLLEAGUE STORIES:
Finding Community

In the absence of willing successors, board members must consider their options. Having no children to carry out his charitable intent, Ray Smith needed to examine his options for the Ray C. Smith Foundation, which he originally established in perpetuity. One option he considered was the Community Foundation for Southeastern Michigan. He found that the community foundation had goals similar to his own—improving the Detroit metropolitan area. This made Smith feel comfortable, and in 1994, two years prior to his death, he signed the foundation over to create a donor-advised fund at the community foundation. The Smith Foundation's three other board members remain as lifetime advisors to the fund. After their service ends, the community foundation's board will make a decision regarding the donor's wishes. The process of rolling a family foundation over into a community foundation is a simple alternative to spending down.

Becoming a Supporting Organization

Although a family foundation could terminate into almost any type of public charity, the most common application of this rule is termination into a supporting organization. A supporting organization is one that achieves its status as a public charity by operating to benefit a larger public charity.

A family foundation can also end its status as a private foundation by becoming a "supporting organization" to a public charity (including a community foundation). Family foundations that choose this option continue to exist as separate 501(c)(3) entities but may choose to relinquish some or all administrative responsibilities. In the simplest model, the nonprofit organization appoints more than 50 percent of the board to the family foundation, which then controls all foundation functions. The rules governing the creation of supporting organizations are very complex, and the foundation should always get advice from its attorney.

An important point to consider when restructuring into a supporting ˙ organization is that disqualified persons may not directly or indirectly control the supporting organization. Accordingly, family members may not hold more than 49 percent of the votes on the supporting organization's board or have a veto power over its decisions.

Termination under this provision takes a minimum of five years. The process begins with a notice to the Internal Revenue Service that the foundation is terminating into a supporting organization to a public charity. The foundation then must continually meet all applicable requirements for public charity status for a period of 60 months from the first day of a taxable year. Because of the long time involved, it is customary to seek an advance ruling from the Internal Revenue Service that the foundation can be expected to successfully complete the termination process.

Spending Down

Foundations may derive a great deal of gratification from simply giving away the total assets of a family foundation. Board members select one or more public charities to receive the corpus directly either as a donation to operations or to support an endowment. When the foundation chooses to spend down, it will grant all of its assets, file appropriate dissolution documents with state and federal governments and cease to exist.

In Their Own Words

Spending Down?
Tell Grantees in Advance

"The CM/Raquel H. Newman Charitable Trust formed in 1973 when my first husband died. I decided to spend down the $2 million trust about five years ago. The impetus for doing this was that I wanted to make two very large gifts and couldn't do it without spending down. I have four children, all in their 40s, all of whom make their own gifts each year. When I tried to include them in the grantmaking decisions, they viewed the foundation as reflecting their parents' interests and preferences, not their own choices. The foundation isn't big enough to split into four pieces to reflect all of their different interests. Instead of having them fuss over it after I'm gone, I decided to spend the foundation down while I'm here. It has been satisfying because I've been able to witness the effect of a few large gifts, while I'm still alive to see it.

One word of advice when spending down: Tell grantees in advance, particularly those you've funded for a long time, that you cannot support them at the level you did. I'm a great believer that if you've funded an organization for a long time, you don't have to fund it forever. Someone else will step up to fund it; the organization will get along without you. But you don't want to take everything away from them in one fell swoop. I told grantees that I was spending down and made a small parting gift to them (a portion of the grant money they had been receiving). There has been no hostility or disappointment expressed on the part of the grantees for the decision I made."

> —Raquel Newman, The CM/Raquel
> Newman Charitable Trust

"It's been satisfying to witness the effect of some large gifts, while I'm still alive to see it."

—Raquel Newman

The Spending Down Debate

Pros of Perpetuity:

- Creates a lasting legacy where the founder will be remembered by the family and by the public

- Passes along philanthropic values to future generations

- Keeps the extended family together over time

- Creates impact over the long term, leaving money available for tomorrow's problems

- Yields even more support for grantees as endowment grows over time

- Keeps funds available in times of economic downturn—today's surplus can be used for tomorrow's unforeseen needs.

Pros of Terminating:

- Allows the donor to see the full effects of the giving in his or her lifetime

- Prevents future generations funding things the donor would not have liked

- Does not bind future generations to an enterprise that may not interest them, may require significant commitment or may cause differences and conflict

- Creates larger impact in the short term, making a larger difference on the problems of today

- Avoids the administrative costs and labor of running a foundation over time

- Precludes the foundation becoming fragmented, ineffective or irrelevant over time.

COLLEAGUE STORIES:
Two Views on Perpetuity

Be Here Later

Since day one, both Diane Bernstein and her husband, Norman, have encouraged their children's involvement in the Diane and Norman Bernstein Foundation of Washington, DC. Having heard that other family foundations struggled with succession issues, the Bernsteins thought it important to involve their six children at an early age so that their eventual transition to the next generation would be smooth.

Although most grants are made to local recipients, the donors left the mission broad. The directors have agreed to certain criteria for grantmaking, but "while our children share the same values, they do not necessarily emphasize the same interests," says Bernstein. To complicate matters, they are geographically dispersed. In order to overcome some of the geographic hurdles, they are allowed to also pursue their interests in their own hometowns with discretionary funds, providing those grants fit the agreed-upon criteria for foundation grants.

While the areas of interest may change with the times and the place, Bernstein hopes their shared values will still guide the board members' decisions. "Whatever works best for them will be the best way to go. Why would we want to tie their hands now?" she says.

Spend It Now

Claude Rosenberg's views on spending down are not a secret. In his 1994 book, *Wealthy and Wise*, he urged individuals to increase their giving, and to do it sooner rather than later. When he and his wife set up a foundation, they chose the "standard" perpetual structure for the Louise and Claude Rosenberg Foundation. Now, says Claude Rosenberg, he and his wife definitely plan to spend down the foundation themselves. "The sooner, the better," Rosenberg said. "We both feel you're limited as to how you can control things after you're gone. We very much feel we should do the most we can while we're alive." One reason, he added, is that "the best things we've done have had a little bravery to them. The next generation might be more cautious. There's a human tendency to be more conservative about taking risks with someone else's money that you've been entrusted with. Future trustees might feel they can't stick their necks out as much."

While he'd like the grandchildren to know the couple is philanthropic, he says, "the choice we have is to leave more to the children and have them inherit a broken society, or to leave them less money and inherit a better society in which to live their lives."

Excerpt from "Forever Is a Long Time," Foundation News & Commentary, *July/August 2003. Council members can access the full article online at www.foundationnews.com.*

COLLEAGUE STORIES:
How to Close an Office

Lucille Parker Markey, whose estate funded the charitable trust named for her, mandated that all its assets and income would be distributed within 15 years of her death, which came in 1982. Thus, plans for setting up the trust also had to include plans for shutting it down. In addition to different investment and funding strategies, and following federal and state regulations, closing a foundation requires planning for personnel and physical resources too.

On the personnel side, critical tasks included close attention to staffing patterns—given the finite life of the trust—and coordinating individual and institutional needs as the termination date drew near. An early decision by trustees to make fewer but larger grants meant a small staff, supplemented by extensive use of consultants. To attract top quality staff, trustees decided to offer a first-rate benefits program, including a generous pension. In its final year, the trust established a special employee severance pay plan that offered substantial bonuses to employees who stayed through the trust's last day. Substantial legal assistance went into crafting the plan so it would not run afoul of federal pension regulations.

Federal law also dictated some procedures related to disposing of the trust's office equipment, furniture and other materials. In Markey's case, these were fully depreciated by the closing date, so they did not have to be sold or auctioned off. Although these goods could be given to a wide range of individuals and charitable organizations without complications, managers and trustees of the foundation could not accept any asset unless its value was assigned to them as taxable income and noted on their W-2 forms as part of their compensation. And every employee's whole compensation package—including receipt of office equipment—had to be within a reasonable range.

The problem of disposal of some major assets was eased through the use of leases for office space and some equipment that were written to terminate with the close of the trust. Distribution of the rest of the equipment, office supplies and other items, including the library, required varying approaches. Most of the rest of the furniture and equipment was offered first to staff, then to charitable institutions in which the staff had an interest. Remaining items were donated to a program of the Dade County, Florida, Public School System that makes donated materials available to teachers. The to-do list also included such mundane tasks as closing bank accounts and safety deposit boxes, and determining when to close out health, disability, liability and other types of insurance.

Adapted from "Spending Down the Markey Way," by John H. Dickason and Duncan Neuhauser, Foundation News and Commentary, *September/October 1999. For further information, refer to* Terminating and Splitting *in Supplementary Sources.*

TOOL BOX:
Changes in Structure

Questions to Think About

About the Family:

- Does the family have a strong identity that is passed down through the generations?

- Do we have a next generation of board members who are interested in participating?

- What is more important to us—keeping family members interested or keeping our current program focus?

- Should the foundation exist forever or is a limited lifetime more appropriate?

- Would family members be upset if the foundation ceased to exist in 15 years?

- Would it be desirable to "sunset" or close down after a fixed period of years or after the last child or grandchild dies?

About Grantmaking:

- Do we believe it is necessary to operate in perpetuity to have a long-lasting impact? Alternatively, could we have the greatest effect through concentrated spending now?

- Have we accomplished our mission?

- Is the mission still relevant? Will it be in 5 years, 10 years, or 50 years?

- If terminating the foundation should prove desirable, is the board aware of the all the options available?

Options for Terminating

Splitting into separate foundations:

- Enables each family to carry out the foundation legacy in a way that suits its interests and style

- Allows family members to connect with each other without the responsibilities of the foundation.

Transferring to a community foundation (or other public charity):

- Makes funds available as a permanent asset in a specific community, with the option to direct funds beyond the community

- Offers a cost-efficient way to manage investments and grantmaking

- Provides families with grant recommendations from professionals based on the family's expressed interests

- Allows for a fund named for the donor to honor his or her legacy.

Qualifying as a Supporting Organization (or other public charity):

- Continues the founder's legacy by expanding the perspective and expertise of the foundation board

- Shifts a public trust managed by a "private" family to a public trust managed by a group of "public" board members.

Spending Down:

- Commits the foundation's assets to current priorities, using today's resources to address today's problems

- Alleviates the family's responsibility for the public trust

- Enables the family members to connect as family without the business of the foundation.

Steps for Splitting a Foundation

Are you considering splitting into separate foundations according to family branches, individuals, generations, etc.? The following suggestions might help you plan for the various stages of the split:

Step One:
Create a foundation task force charged with negotiating the creation of two or more foundations. The task force might consider using an outside facilitator to mediate.

Step Two:
In the task force, determine how to divide the assets among the different segments.

Step Three:
Engage counsel to prepare the legal documents necessary to establish new corporations/trusts and asset bases.

Step Four:

Each segment engages in a planning process to establish a mission, goals, governance structure, investment and payout policies, grantmaking priorities and processes, identify staffing and/or service needs for its foundation. Negotiate which segment "gets" existing staff (if any), office space and equipment.

The Laws on Terminating

To find out the rules on terminating, see Revenue Ruling 2002-28, which addresses three common private foundation termination scenarios—divorce, merger and conversion from trust to corporation—or Revenue Ruling 2003-13, which addresses termination to public charities.

There are three common ways to terminate a private foundation without paying the termination tax imposed under Section 507 of the Internal Revenue Code. First, the foundation may distribute all of its assets to existing public charities, including community foundations. Second, the foundation may become a public charity. Finally, the foundation may transfer its assets to another private foundation. For more information about the laws on terminating, contact the Council on Foundations Legal Services staff at legal@cof.org.

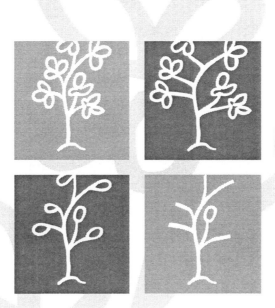

Part 3

Samples

COUNCIL *on* FOUNDATIONS

Board Development
and Structure

Many family foundations set qualifications for membership on their board.
Virtually all set a minimum age requirement for participation, and those that
allow lifetime appointments often impose a maximum age for retirement as well.
Some foundations list additional qualifications family members must meet before
they can be nominated, including knowledge of funding areas, knowledge of legal
or financial matters, volunteer experience or familiarity with the geographic
regions served.

Eligibility Criteria to Consider for Board Service

	Candidate Qualities	Qualities Sought by Board
Demographic Diversity		
Age		
Community Representative		
Gender		
Location		
Family (or nonfamily) Status		
Generation represented		
Personal Skills		
Strategic Thinker/Strategic Planning		
Problem-Solver		
Team Builder		
Visionary		
Asks good questions		
Open-minded		
Passionate about philanthropy		
Good speaker/presenter		
Strong facilitation skills		
Cultivates relationships		
Works well in groups		
Time management skills		
Conflict resolution skills		

Continued on page 124

Eligibility Criteria to Consider for Board Service (cont.)

	Candidate Qualities	Qualities Sought by Board
Personal Skills (cont.)		
Willing to develop relationships with grantees		
Good written communication skills		
Technology		
Other skills		
Professional Skills		
Accounting/Finance		
Administrative Management		
Attorney/Legal		
Funding Area Expertise		
Government/Legislative/Advocacy		
Investments/Finance		
Marketing/Public Relations		
Media/Journalism		
Nonprofit		
Technology		
Other		
Grantmaking Experience & Knowledge		
Advocacy		
Capacity Building/Technical Assistance		
Collaborations		
Community Building		
Evaluation		
Other		
Philanthropic Experience		
Foundation Committee Service		
Foundation Junior or Advisory Board		
Other Nonprofit Board Service		
Philanthropic Networks (e.g., affinity group, regional association, Council on Foundations		
Philanthropic Education (conferences/seminars)		
Volunteer Service in the Community		

Sample Bylaws

Courtesy of the Merrick Foundation

Article III
Section 3.2   *Classes, Qualifications, and Terms of Trustees*

There shall be three (3) classes of Trustees, as follows:

(a) Class I Trustees. Class I Trustees shall be members of the Ward S. Merrick, Sr. family (which for purposes herein shall include only lineal descendants of Ward S. Merrick, Sr. born or adopted into the line of descent). Up to eight (8) members of the Ward S. Merrick, Sr. family may serve as Class I Trustees. Of these eight members, no more than four (4) Class I Trustees may be members of the Elizabeth Merrick Coe branch of the family (which for purposes herein shall include Elizabeth Merrick Coe and any lineal descendants of hers born or adopted into the line of descent) and no more than four (4) Class I Trustees may be members of the Ward S. Merrick, Jr. branch of the family (which for purposes herein shall include Ward S. Merrick, Jr. and any lineal descendant of Ward S. Merrick, Jr. born or adopted into the line of descent). Each Class I Trustee must be not younger than age twenty-five (25) nor older than age seventy-five (75). Each Class I Trustee shall serve for a term of one (1) year, subject to reelection without limitation.

(b) Class II Trustees. Class II Trustees shall be persons who are not members of the Ward S. Merrick, Sr. family, who are not related to any member of the Ward S. Merrick, Sr. family, and who are not married to any member of or any person who is related to any member of the Ward S. Merrick, Sr. family. It is preferable, although not required, that Class II Trustees be residents of Ardmore, Oklahoma, who are active in community affairs, knowledgeable about south central Oklahoma, and who understand the mission and share the philanthropic values of the Merrick family. Each Class II Trustee shall serve for a three (3) year term, subject to reelection. However, any Class II Trustee who has served for two (2) full three-year terms may not be reelected until the expiration of one (1) year from the date of the end of that person's most recent term of service. Notwithstanding the foregoing, the Trustees may elect Class II Trustees to initial terms of longer than three (3) years on a staggered basis in order to implement the provisions hereof.

(c) Associate Trustees. Class I Trustees representing one of the two branches of the Ward S. Merrick, Sr. family may nominate members of that branch of the family for election as Associate Trustees. Associate Trustees must meet the same qualification requirements as Class I Trustees. *There shall be no limit on the number of Associate Trustees serving at any time. All Associate trustees will be elected for a one-year term subject to reelection without limitation.* Associate Trustees shall have the right to attend meetings of the Trustees and to sit on committees of the Trustees if and when appointed. However, Associate Trustees shall have no voting rights or other rights as a Trustee except as expressly set forth in these Bylaws or as agreed upon by the Trustees.

All references to Trustees in these Bylaws shall refer to Class I and Class II Trustees only.

Courtesy of the Emily Hall Tremaine Foundation, Inc.

Article IV   Board of Directors
Section 4.2   *Number and Qualifications*

(a) Number. The Board shall be composed of a minimum of five (5) and a maximum of sixteen (16) Directors elected to office pursuant to these Bylaws ("Elected Directors") and ex officio Directors and emeritus Directors to the extent provided in these Bylaws. Not less than two-thirds (2/3) of the Elected Directors shall be Descendants (as hereinafter defined) of Burton G. Tremaine (1901–1991) for so long as there are a sufficient number of such Descendants who are willing, able and qualified to serve as Elected Directors in the opinion of seventy percent (70%) of the Voting Directors (as defined in Section 4.3(a)) then in office. "Descendants" shall include blood descendants and their spouses, children and their issue who are legally adopted by blood descendants and the spouses of such persons, and stepchildren of blood descendants who join the family before age nineteen (19), and the spouses and the issue of such persons. For purposes of this Section, Burton G. Tremaine, Jr.'s stepson, Atwood Collins III, is deemed to have joined the family before age nineteen (19). A Descendant and his or her spouse may serve simultaneously. The Board shall have the power to fix its number within such maximum or minimum by resolution without amendment to these bylaws. Unless the Board acts to reduce or increase the number of Elected Directors, the number of Elected Directors shall be the number elected at the last Annual Meeting of the Board. Notwithstanding any other provision of these Bylaws, the number of Elected Directors shall never be fixed at a number fewer than the number of persons qualified to serve as Branch Heads, in accordance with Section 4.2(e), as determined by the Governance Committee. It shall not be a qualification of office that Elected Directors be residents of the State of Connecticut. Should these Bylaws be amended to limit the number of consecutive terms that may be served by Elected Directors, those Elected Directors elected prior to January 1, 1992 (the "Founding Directors") shall be exempt from such limitation. If a Founding Director elects to take a leave of absence and subsequently wishes to be reelected to the Board at a time when no vacancy exists, such Founding Director shall have priority over any others for consideration for the next available vacancy which he or she is qualified to fill and may serve as an ex officio Director until such a vacancy occurs.

(b) Age Limitations. To be eligible for election to the Board, an individual first elected after the adoption of these Bylaws must be at least twenty-five (25) years of age, but less than seventy (70) years of age, except for Founding Directors Burton G. Tremaine, Jr. (b. 1922) and Dorothy Tremaine Hildt (b. 1927), who may each stand for election until seventy-five (75) years of age. The age limitations included in this Section 4.2(b) may be waived by the affirmative vote of seventy percent (70%) of the Voting Directors with respect to any incumbent Director who the Governance Committee recommends be invited to stand for reelection. Any such waiver shall be reconsidered annually.

(c) Ex Officio Directors. The President of the Foundation shall be an ex officio member of the Board. An Immediate Past Chair shall also serve as an ex officio Director, as set forth in Section 5.4(b) of these Bylaws. A Founding Director returning from a leave of absence and awaiting the occurrence of a vacancy on the Board pursuant to Section 4.2(a) may serve as an ex officio Director. Ex officio Directors shall have all rights of other members of the Board, including full voting rights on all matters coming before the Board except that the President shall not vote on any Major Matter as defined in Section 4.5(b)(2) and shall not be counted as a Voting Director for purposes of Section 4.5(b)(2).

(d) Emeritus Directors. The Board shall have the power to confer emeritus status on any retiring Director upon a finding by the Board that the retiring Director has rendered exceptional and distinguished service to the Foundation. Emeritus Directors shall be entitled to receive notice of and to attend all Board meetings and to participate fully in all Board discussions, but they shall not have any voting rights on matters considered by the Board.

(e) Branches. Branch Heads and At-Large Directors. Except as otherwise provided in these Bylaws, seven (7) of the Elected Directors shall be elected as branch heads ("Branch Heads") of the following branches (each individually a "Branch") of the family of Burton G. Tremaine (1901–1991), listed by age: the Atwood Collins III Branch; the Burton G. Tremaine III Branch; the John McGean Tremaine Branch; the Janet Carleton Tremaine Stanley Branch; the Sarah Chapman Tremaine Branch; the Dorothy Wick DePetro Branch; and the Kenneth Bryant Wick, Jr. Branch. The members of each Branch qualified to be considered for election as a Branch Head shall consist of the aforementioned person, such person's spouse, and such person's Descendants (as defined in Section 4.2(a). If at any time the Governance Committee determines that a Branch has no member who is willing, able and qualified to serve as its Branch Head, a member of another Branch may be elected. Any Director so elected and any other Elected Directors in addition to Branch Heads shall be at-large Directors ("At-Large Directors"). Notwithstanding any other provision of these Bylaws, not more than one Elected Director shall be a member of the same Branch at any time that the number of Elected Directors, including vacancies, is six (6) or fewer, not more than two (2) of the Elected Directors, shall be members of the same Branch at any time that the number of Elected Directors, including vacancies, is more than six (6) and fewer than eleven (11), and not more than three (3) of the Elected Directors shall be members of the same Branch at any time that the number of Elected Directors, including vacancies, is eleven (11) or more.

(f) Service as an Associate Director. On and after June 24, 1999, no Elected Director shall be elected who has not served at least two (2) one-year terms as an Associate Director; provided, however, that the foregoing limitation may be waived by the affirmative vote of seventy percent (70%) of the Voting Directors.

(g) Service as an Associate Director and/or At-Large Director. No Branch Head shall be elected who has not served a total of four (4) years as an Associate Director and/or At-Large Director, provided, however, that the foregoing limitation may be waived by the affirmative vote of seventy percent (70%) of the Voting Directors.

Courtesy of The Nathan Cummings Foundation, Inc.

Article III Board of Trustees

Number and Qualifications

Number. The Board shall be composed of a minimum of six members and a maximum of fifteen members. At all times, no less than a simple majority of the members of the Board will be members of the Nathan Cummings Family, provided that there are a sufficient number of family members who are willing, able, and qualified to serve as Trustees. For purposes of this Section, the Nathan Cummings family shall be defined as follows: Beatrice Cummings Mayer, her descendants, and the spouses of such descendants; the lineal descendants of Herbert K. Cummings, deceased, and their spouses; and the lineal descendants of Alan H. Cummings, deceased, and their spouses. In the event of a family member marrying a person with children, those children will be treated as members of the Nathan Cummings Family if they are adopted.

Branch Representation. There will be at least one family member from each branch on the Board if there is a family member willing and qualified to serve. If the only member of a branch is about to go off the Board, the Trustees and Associates in that branch will recommend a new branch member for consideration by the Governance Committee for Board membership. In all other cases, the Governance Committee will recommend new family Trustees to the Board without branch recommendation.

Election, Tenure, Resignation and Removal

Election; Term of Office. Trustees will be elected to initial terms of three years. Family Trustees may be reelected after each three-year term. Non-family Trustees may be elected to serve a second three-year term, after which there will be a minimum of one year off the Board. Former Board members need not serve as Associates before being considered by the Governance Committee for Board membership, and they may be considered after they have been off the Board for one year.

Removal. …In the event of a *divorce*, the term of a divorced spouse of a family member as a Trustee will terminate at the time of divorce. In the event of the *death of a family member*, the surviving spouse will continue as a family member as defined in Section 3.2(a). If the surviving spouse remarries, the subsequent spouse will not be considered a family member, but the surviving spouse will continue as a family member. If the surviving spouse marries and has children, the children will not be considered family members. In the event of a *separation*, if Foundation work is adversely affected by the separation, the Governance Committee will be authorized to recommend to the Board the removal of the spouse of a family member as Trustee.

Sample Membership Structure: The Two-Tiered Board

Some boards create a membership structure, which distinguishes between two or more levels of board involvement and voting rights. Below is just one sample of how such a structure can be designed.

Members:

1. Are lineal descendents of the founder by birth

2. Are at least 40 years of age

3. Have served as trustees for at least one year.

New members are elected by a majority of current members and have the authority to amend the Articles of Incorporation; to approve a merger, consolidation, reorganization or dissolution of the Foundation; to elect members of the Foundation; and to elect and remove Trustees of the Foundation.

Trustees:

1. Are lineal descendents of the founder by birth

2. Are at least 30 years of age

3. Have demonstrated interest in the Foundation.

Trustees are elected by a majority of those serving as Members, and have the authority to act on any business not reserved to Members as described above. Under normal circumstances, this means that Trustees are authorized to vote on everything except election of Members and Trustees. They may vote on grants, on approval of administrative expenses, etc. Those who do not meet the eligibility requirements listed above may nonetheless be elected as Trustees by a unanimous vote of those serving as Members. This would allow for election of spouses or nonfamily members as Trustees.

Sample Term Limit and Rotation Policy

Many family foundations impose term limits on board members, limiting the length of terms and/or the number of consecutive terms a member may serve.

The board of directors shall consist of seven (7) members. In addition to the two (2) original donors, five (5) of these will be family, defined as direct descendants of the foundation's original donors. Original donors will serve life appointments. Aside from the original donors, only those family members who are 21 or older and 75 and younger are eligible to serve on the board. These family members will serve two-year terms on a rotating basis. After one two-year term has been served, the board member must step off the board for a period of two years, upon which time he or she will again be eligible for nomination. The current board must vote by majority rule in order for that family member to be reelected. The grandchildren will serve two-year terms on a rotating basis. The rotation of grandchildren serving on the board is determined by age beginning with the oldest grandchild. Each grandchild must be 21 before he or she is elected to the board. Minor children will enter the rotation on their 21st birthdays.

Two (2) of the board members will be from the community, will not be direct descendants of the donor, and will serve a maximum of two (2) consecutive three-year terms.

Sample Process for Selecting New Board Members

Courtesy of the Mary Reynolds Babcock Foundation

1. Answer the questions: *"What do we want the board to be like? What skills, characteristics, knowledge and experiences do we want in the group as a whole?"* Using its answers to this question, the board then analyzes what is missing on the current board, decides specific criteria for Directors to be recruited, and agrees on examples of the types of people for whom to search. (This is done by the full board at a regular board meeting.)

2. Conduct a broad search for candidates who fit the criteria.

   a) Contact a variety of resources to get recommendations of people who fit the criteria.

   b) Solicit names regularly, at least once a year, from current Directors.

   c) Develop a network of resource people who are involved in effective community change (including some of our current grant recipients) from whom we can request names of candidates who fit our stated criteria.

   d) Staff follows up recommendations with requests for vitae and compiles a database.

3. Circulate the list of candidates and vitae material to all Directors. (In 1995, we collected vitae on 53 recommended people.)

4. Review candidates and choose a few to interview. (Done by the full board at a regular board meeting.)

5. Interview candidates. (Done by Nominating Committee)

6. Nominating Committee nominates Directors for election at the annual Members Meeting.

Every two years, revisit the make-up of the board and specific criteria for new members, making adjustments in the search criteria as necessary.

Sample Discussion Worksheet:
Expanding the Board Beyond Family

Considering bringing on nonfamily board members? Use this sample as a discussion worksheet for your board. A similar format may be used for almost any issue facing your foundation.

Things that may change	Hopes	Fears	Possible Solutions
Geographic focus			
Purpose/mission			
Size			
History/legacy			
Grantmaking			
Board dynamics			
Responsiveness			
Control			
Diversity			
Quality of discussion			
Justice			
Privacy			
Other?			

Board Member Responsibilities and Evaluation

Sample Responsibilities for Overall Board

Not necessarily in priority order

1. Establish and amend the Foundation's bylaws.

2. Elect its Directors, Officers and Committees.

3. Select, oversee, counsel and assess its President.

4. Establish and safeguard the Foundation's vision and mission.

5. Establish and safeguard its values.

6. Ensure its long-term strength and vibrancy as a family endeavor.

7. Ensure legal, ethical and financial integrity and effective resource management.

   a. Establish and oversee investment policies; select asset managers.

   b. Establish and oversee administrative policies and budget.

8. Set high grantmaking goals; ensure their creative and effective achievement.

   a. Determine program grantmaking focus.

   b. Co-create and monitor program strategies.

   c. Determine discretionary grant policy.

9. Allocate distribution of administrative, program and discretionary funds.

10. Periodically assess the Board's strategies, decisions, strengths, needs and performance.

Sample Responsibilities
for Individual Board Members

Not necessarily in priority order

1. Commit to the Foundation's vision and mission.

2. Exemplify and uphold its values.

3. Serve the interests of the Foundation as a whole.

4. Maintain a working knowledge of the Foundation's finances, operations, program and legal framework.

5. Faithfully attend and prepare for Board and Committee meetings.

6. Fully and openly participate in Board and Committee deliberations.

   a. Ask with an open and curious mind.

   b. Respect, listen and learn from others.

   c. Maintain independence and objectivity; advocate according to conviction.

   d. Strive toward consensus; respect and represent majority decisions.

7. Actively collaborate in the creation of program strategies.

8. Positively represent the Foundation to the public.

9. Engage and inform family members about stewardship, philanthropy and service.

10. Honor family dignity and integrity.

Sample Board Member Job Description 1

Courtesy of the Leighty Foundation

Board Members:

- Determine, articulate and support the purpose and mission of the Foundation.

- Elect the Board and determine the bylaws of the Foundation.

- Attend the meetings of the Board by conference call or in person.

- Ensure that the Foundation functions within appropriate legal and fiscal constraints.
- Research funding opportunities in areas of interest of the Foundation.
- Initiate relationships with potential grantees.
- Serve as advocates for the cause of potential grantees.
- Conduct site visits.
- Participate in grant follow-ups and evaluations (if not a staff function).
- Build relationships and collaborate with other funders.
- Review investment philosophy and investment opportunities for the Foundation.
- Engage in lifelong learning in areas of interest and expertise.
- Serve as catalysts for information sharing.
- Assist each other as requested.

Sample Board Member Job Description 2

Courtesy of the W. Clement & Jessie V. Stone Foundation

Trustees act as voting members of the Board with full authority and responsibility to develop policies, procedures and regulations for the operation of the Foundation and to monitor the Foundation's financial health, programs and overall performance.

Policy:

- To make a final determination and vote on the strategic plan for the Foundation, and to evaluate the Foundation's performance in accomplishing its mission on an annual basis.
- To review, discuss and vote on Program Committee guidelines, and to vote on all grant submissions for funding.
- To develop policies for the operation of the Program Committees, and to develop policies for trustee participation on the Board.

Personnel:

- To hire the Executive Director, determine performance standards and evaluate performance on an annual basis.
- To review and approve personnel policies.

Finance:

- To review and approve the Foundation's annual budget.
- To annually review and implement both the spending policy, which determines the amount of money that will be available for grantmaking, and the investment policy that fulfills the mission and goals of the Foundation.
- To oversee the work of the Finance Committee in defining investment goals, in monitoring the management of investments, and in adhering to tax requirements.

Sample Board Member Self-Evaluation

Here is one example of a self-evaluation tool for board members.

	Strongly Agree				Strongly Disagree
1. I understand and support the mission of the foundation.	5	4	3	2	1
2. I understand my roles and responsibilities.	5	4	3	2	1
3. I monitor developments and trends in the field.	5	4	3	2	1
4. I serve effectively on the board.	5	4	3	2	1
5. I prepare in advance, regularly attend and actively participate in meetings.	5	4	3	2	1

	Strongly Agree				Strongly Disagree
6. I read and understand the foundation's financial statements.	5	4	3	2	1
7. I volunteer for committees and serveeffectively on them.	5	4	3	2	1
8. I recommend individuals for service on this board.	5	4	3	2	1
9. I express my thoughts and opinions and believe they are heard and considered.	5	4	3	2	1
10. I communicate the value of philanthropy and this foundation to policymakers, other grantmakers, the media and the general public when given the opportunity.	5	4	3	2	1

11. Do you find board service to be a valuable and rewarding experience? Why or why not?

12. What would improve your effectiveness as a board member?

13. If you disagreed with any of the above statements, please explain.

14. What could the foundation do to better support the board as a whole?

15. Additional comments.

Sample Board Member Performance Evaluation

The Blandin Foundation in Grand Rapids, Minnesota, created a peer review process in 1997 to measure board performance. Each board member completes a questionnaire that evaluates fellow board members. The questionnaire focuses on four areas:

1. Knowledge of and commitment to the foundation
2. Relationship skills
3. Board-level performance
4. Recommendation for re-nomination.

Once the questionnaires have been completed, the board chair meets individually with each board member to share the results. For more information, read the June/July 1998 issue of *Foundation News & Commentary* at www.cof.org/foundationnews/backissues.htm or contact the Blandin Foundation at www.blandinfoundation.org.

Donor Intent and Death of the Donor

Sample Letter of Donor Intent

Courtesy of H.D. (Ike) Leighty, The Leighty Foundation, July 1999

I have yet to meet a donor or founder of a charitable foundation who said, "When I started out, my goal was to make a lot of money so I could give it away."

When I began to realize that I was accumulating more money than I needed, or could reasonably spend, I started to plan to use it to help others. Why? Because of my upbringing—the love, caring and sharing experience from my family; my church and the Christian way of life and what it teaches about service to others; and people like Mother Moon.

I set up the Foundation in 1986 to "park" up to 50 percent of my income each year while I was deciding where He wanted me to put it to use helping those in need.

My original intent? To do good—whatever that means....

By inviting Bill and Jane, and later Nancy and Bob, to help to find worthy causes for the funds generated by the Foundation investments, I also visualized it as an opportunity to draw our widespread family closer together.

As the Foundation and our roles in it have evolved, we have become aware and sensitive to our diverse interests, which can offer challenges as well as opportunities to use as a family.

My intent has evolved from just "doing good" to the creation of our current mission statement:

"To carry on the Leighty family legacy of service and stewardship by leveraging our time, talents and finances primarily in the areas of science and the environment, education, spirituality, women's interests, human population, peacemaking, volunteerism and the promotion of philanthropy."

When we first started, Bill posed the question, "There is so much need out there, why don't we give it all away—put it in the hands of those who can place it where it will do the most good *now*?"

Good question! I would suggest it be posed and answered at the start of every annual meeting of the Leighty Foundation. We should always be willing to consider a sunset date for the Foundation as an alternative to maintaining it in perpetuity.

I believe the Lord entrusted me with the stewardship of this portion of His great bounty to give me a challenge and opportunity to use it to develop and practice my concern for others—to use me to put His arms around those in need. That has become my intent.

I have invited my family to participate in the stewardship of this challenge and opportunity. Notice that it is not the H.D. Leighty Foundation—it is the Leighty [family] Foundation.

In joining me, the family has received the side benefit of the opportunity to work and draw closer together, and to meet and get to know others who are challenged with similar opportunities—a great group of worthwhile people.

It is my intent that we make donations and support causes where our comparatively small amounts of money can be used as leverage—seed money—to attract other givers to the cause or project—like the Parable of the Mustard Seed!

It is also my intent that we leverage the time, talent and experience we develop in the members of our family to mentor other potential donors as they discover the joy of giving their share of His great bounty—to help them establish and grow their own family philanthropy.

I would like us to be "philanthropic missionaries" and regularly allocate a portion of our funds to emphasize and support that part of our mission.

My family is my #1 interest!

I hope that they grow together as stewards of all our family gene pools as well as the Foundation. If at some time in the future, the operation and administration of the Foundation should be in danger of splitting the family apart, it would be my intention that the Foundation and the stewardship of its assets be given to an independent agency such as the Community Foundation of Waterloo and NE Iowa to administer. I have full confidence in my family's ability to choose wisely regarding both the health of the family and the stewardship of the Foundation.

Sample Obituary

John Robert Smith passed away peacefully at the Memorial Hospital at 2 p.m. on Friday, January 17, 2003, at age 66. John was the loving husband of 30 years to Mary, and father of Peter, 22 and Karen, 20.

John will be remembered most notably for his great contributions to the community in which he was born and lived. As founder of the Smith Family Foundation formed in 1983, John was committed to eliminating domestic violence in New County by supporting direct service organizations and shelters—both through the foundation and through his own personal giving. Under John's leadership, the foundation contributed more than $5 million to nonprofit service providers countywide. Before his retirement, John ran Smith Tough Tires, the family tire manufacturing business started by his father in 1954.

Visitation will be 3–5 p.m. and 7–9 p.m. on Monday, January 20 at the Memory Funeral Home, 156 Willow Street. The funeral will take place at 11 a.m. on Tuesday, January 21 at St. Paul's Church, followed by a burial ceremony at Birchview Cemetery. Memorial donations may be made to the New County Domestic Violence Shelter.

Sample Press Release

News releases should be printed on your foundation's letterhead. They should be double-spaced and printed on one side of the page only. Below is an example that shows how to format a news release.

FOR IMMEDIATE RELEASE
(DATE)

CONTACT: (NAME OF FOUNDATION OR FAMILY MEMBER)
(TITLE)
(PHONE)

FOUNDER OF SMITH FAMILY FOUNDATION DIES

New County, AK—John Robert Smith, the founder of the 20-year-old Smith Family Foundation, died peacefully today at 2 p.m. in the Memorial Hospital. He was surrounded by his loved ones— his wife of 30 years, Mary, and children Peter, 22, and Karen, 20.

With a vision to end domestic violence in New County, Smith founded the Smith Family Foundation with his wife Mary in 1983. Under his leadership, the foundation contributed more than $5 million to nonprofit service providers countywide. According to Joan Edwards, executive director of the Arkansas Domestic Violence Coalition, "John's contribution to eliminating domestic violence goes beyond the dollars his foundation granted. He gave his time and energy to promoting programs and advocacy that improved the lives of all victims of violence in New County." His wife, children and two community board members will carry on the work of the foundation according to John's mission to help victims, continuing the legacy that he envisioned.

Before his work with the foundation, Smith ran Smith Tough Tires, the family tire manufacturing business started by his father in 1954. He earned an MBA from the University of Arkansas in 1962.

Visitation will be 3–5 p.m. and 7–9 p.m. on Monday, January 20 at the Memory Funeral Home, 156 Willow Street. The funeral will take place at 11 a.m. on Tuesday, January 21 at St. Paul's Church, followed by a burial ceremony at Birchview Cemetery. The family recommends memorial donations be made to the New County Domestic Violence Shelter.

Sample Memorial Document

Courtesy of The Charles and Lynn Schusterman Family Foundation

Inaugural Report 1987–2001
Message from the President
Lynn Schusterman, December 2001

Publishing an annual report is something many of us at the Foundation have wanted to do for several years. Each time the idea came before our board, however, the same person asked us to wait a little longer: my late husband, Charles Schusterman. "Because," he told us, "we're not ready."

To Charlie, being ready meant understanding the broadest outlines and smallest details of every issue. He always wanted to gather and analyze as much data as possible before making a decision or taking action.

His unquenchable thirst for knowledge and love of people led Charlie from boardrooms to classrooms, and from conferences to conversations into which he would draw those around him. He particularly enjoyed talking to young people, believing they possess a unique perspective on how to build for the future. And not only did he go and see and do, Charlie also read everything he could, always chiding himself for lacking discipline whenever he stuffed a nonessential publication into his briefcase to read at night or over the weekend. Charlie embodied information overload, as anyone who ever saw the piles of newspapers, magazines and industry newsletters he kept at our home and in his office can attest.

In the midst of all this activity, however, stood a focused man with a keen mind and relentless drive. He was deservedly and universally respected for his ability to assess and manage risk, a talent he displayed over and over again when confronted with new and daunting challenges in every aspect of his extraordinary life—in business, in philanthropy, and ultimately, in battling two diseases.

Despite these illnesses and the debilitating side effects that followed, Charlie vigorously pursued a two-pronged philanthropic agenda with goals that were both visionary and achievable. First and foremost, Charlie wanted to ensure that a critical mass of engaged Jews live in North America in the 21st century and beyond. Only then, he was convinced, could his beloved Jewish people continue to have a positive impact on the world—to truly serve as a "light unto the nations."

Charlie also felt a special loyalty to his hometown. He was deeply committed to helping local organizations that shared his desire to help people improve their skills and build better lives. By the time he died last December, our family had already pledged more than $50 million toward the two objectives Charlie had set for us in the early 1990s—over half of which was committed in just the last two years. The table around which we made our funding decisions had moved from our kitchen to a downtown office, and the people making those decisions had grown to include the members of our experienced professional staff. Charlie's innermost thoughts about philanthropy and life, as well as the lessons he learned during his endless quest for knowledge, had been communicated to those of us he knew would survive him. And, for at least the next few years, our course had been charted. Thanks to Charlie, we're ready.

Conclusion

COUNCIL *on* FOUNDATIONS

Conclusion

Working in a family foundation means facing many challenges. The challenges of change are not easy, and sometimes can escalate into crises that can leave the family wondering: "Why are we doing this?" "How long should the foundation stay in operation?" "Is it still a benefit to the family, or has it become a burden?" These are important questions to ask yourselves, no matter the age of your foundation.

It helps to remember why your foundation came together in the first place. Ask yourself, *What are we trying to create?* Most family foundations converge with a shared sense of purpose—to perpetuate a legacy, to solidify the family, to help others, to do good in the world. In times of change, challenge and conflict, remember the reasons why your family foundation exists and why it is important to each one of you to resolve the issues at hand.

No one has the answers to every difficult situation your foundation may encounter. Besides, the answers today may be different in five years. Your board doesn't need to find permanent solutions to these hard questions, but it does need to have the discussions. Good board discussions can influence how your foundation does business—its governance, its management and its grantmaking. If, as a result of these discussions, your board develops policies and practices, it will mitigate the family tension that arises during times of pressure. Board and family members will learn through advance discussions where their values

In times of change, challenge and conflict, remember the reasons why your family foundation exists, and why it is important to each one of you to resolve the issues at hand.

align and where they do not. You may find that some beliefs they assumed are shared are in fact not, and that some perceived personal differences are just that—perceptions. You may also learn how different board members would choose to respond to different challenges, before the challenge arises.

With so many challenges, conflicts and potential crises, what's the good news for family foundations? Simply this: challenges and change can bring the foundation board closer through shared experience and common goals. Not everyone will have the same response to a particular challenge, but challenges illuminate the environment of support, love and collectivity that is central to the family foundation enterprise. Challenges can bring enormous opportunity for family foundations to raise profound questions about themselves, both as individuals and as a family unit, and to make decisions about how the foundation will manage change for the good of all involved.

Book In Sum
A Successful Family Foundation:

- Knows and communicates its core values and purpose
- Has a mission and goals that guide its grantmaking
- Makes an impact in the community and focus areas it serves.
- Follows its legal, fiduciary and ethical responsibilities
- Plans ahead for the future
- Prepares for changes and challenges
- Bases decisions on policy, not personal likes and dislikes
- Has members who interact well, make decisions together, and enjoy the dual family and working relationships
- Actively engages each member
- Evaluates its own work

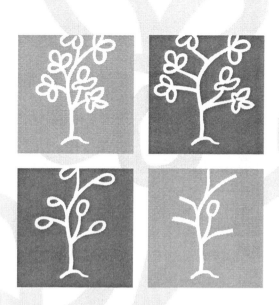

Supplementary Sources

COUNCIL *on* FOUNDATIONS

Supplementary Sources

Read More

Boards

The Board Building Cycle. Sandra Hughes, Berit Lakey and Marla Bobowick. BoardSource (formerly National Center for Nonprofit Boards), 2000. To order, call 800/883-6262 or visit www.boardsource.org.

The Family Advisor: Board Composition. Council on Foundations. To order, call 202/467-0407 or e-mail family@cof.org.

Family Foundation Retreat Guide. Council on Foundations. To order, call 888/239-5221, order #808 or visit www.cof.org.

Foundation Trusteeship: Service in the Public Interest. The Foundation Center, 1989. To order, call 888/239-5221, order # 404 or visit www.cof.org.

A Founder's Guide to the Family Foundation: How to Use, Govern and Enjoy Your Family Foundation. Council on Foundations, 1994. To order call 888/239-5221, order #813 or visit www.cof.org.

Governance: Family Foundation Library series. Council on Foundations, 1997. To order call 888/239-5221, order #816 or visit www.cof.org.

Governance Series. BoardSource, 2003. To order call 800/883-6262 or visit www.boardsource.org.

Voyage of Discovery: A Planning Workbook for Philanthropic Families. Healey, Judith. National Center for Family Philanthropy, 2001. To order, call 202/393-3424 or visit www.ncfp.org.

"What Makes Great Boards Great," Jeffrey A. Sonnenfeld. *Harvard Business Review*, September 2002, pp. 106–113.

Ways Your Family Foundation Can Grow and Thrive. The Family Foundation Series. Council of Michigan Foundations, 1997. To order, visit www.cmif.org.

Board Member Orientation

The Family Advisor: Trustee Orientation. Council on Foundations. To order, call 202/467-0407 or e-mail family@.cof.org.

The Trustee Notebook: An Orientation for Family Foundation Board Members. Robert Hull. National Center for Family Philanthropy, 1999. To order, call 202/393-3424 or visit www.ncfp.org.

Trustee Orientation Resource. Council on Foundations, 1993. To order, call 888/239-5221, order #403 or visit www.cof.org.

Conflict of Interest

Ethical Choices for Family Foundations. Institute for Global Ethics, 2001. To order call 888/239-5221, order #824 or visit www.cof.org.

"Conflict of Interest," *Family Matters,* Summer 1996. Council on Foundations. Members can access online at www.cof.org.

Managing Conflicts of Interest: Practical Guidelines for Nonprofit Boards. Daniel Kurtz. BoardSource (formerly National Center for Nonprofit Boards), 2001. To order call 800/883-6262 or visit www.boardsource.org.

Responsible Family Philanthropy: A Resource Book on Ethical Decisionmaking for Family Foundations. Michael Rion. Council on Foundations, 1998. To order, call 888/239-5221, order #854 or visit www.cof.org.

Consultants

Resources for Family Philanthropy: Finding the Best People, Advice, and Support. National Center Journal, Volume 1. National Center for Family Philanthropy, 1999. To order, call 202/293-3424 or visit www.ncfp.org.

Succeeding With Consultants: Self-Assessment for the Changing Nonprofit. Barbara Kibbe and Fred Setterberg. Foundation Center, 1992. To order, call 800/424-9836 or visit www.fdncenter.org.

Dealing with Differences

Keeping the Peace: Resolving Conflict in the Boardroom. Marion Peters Angelica. BoardSource (formerly National Center for Nonprofit Boards) and the Amherst H. Wilder Foundation, 2000. To order, visit www.wilder.org/pubs.

Family Meetings: How to Build a Stronger Family and a Stronger Business.
Family Business Leadership Series, No. 2. Craig E. Aronoff and John L. Ward.
Georgia: Business Owner Resources, 1992. To order, call 800/551-0633.

The Troublesome Board Member. Mark Bailey. BoardSource, 1996. To order,
call 800/883-6262 or visit www.governance.com.au.

The Collaborative Leadership Handbook: A Guide for Citizens and Civic Leaders.
David C. Chrislip. Jossey-Bass, 2002. To order, visit www.josseybass.com.

How to Make Meetings Work. Michael Doyle and David Straus. Berkeley, California: Berkeley Publishing Group, 1993. To order, visit www.amazon.com.

Getting To Yes: Negotiating Agreement Without Giving In. Roger Fisher and
William Ury. New York: Penguin Books, 1991. To order, visit www.pen-
guinputnam.com or www.amazon.com.

Getting Together: Building Relationships as We Negotiate. Roger Fisher and
Scott Brown. New York: Penguin Books, 1989. To order, visit www.pen-
guinputnam.com or www.amazon.com.

"When Generations Disagree." Scott Frankenberg, et al. *Foundation News
and Commentary*, July/August 2001. www.foundationnews.org.

Working With the Ones You Love: Strategies for a Successful Family Business.
Dennis T. Jaffe. California: Conari Press, 1991.

"Managing Conflicts and Family Dynamics In Your Family's Philanthropy."
Deborah Brody Hamilton. *Passages: Exploring Key Issues in Family Giving,
vol. 4.2.* National Center for Family Philanthropy. www.ncfp.org.

"Family Foundation Feuds." H. Tony Oppenheimer et al. *Foundation News
& Commentary*, January/February 2001. www.foundationnews.org.

Family Issues: Family Foundation Library series. Deanne Stone. Council on
Foundations, 1997. To order, call 888/239-5221, order # 815 or visit
www.cof.org.

Difficult Conversations: How to Discuss What Matters Most. Douglas Stone,
Bruce Patton and Sheila Heen. Viking, 1999.

*I Only Say This Because I Love You: Talking to Your Parents, Partner, Sibs and
Kids When You're All Adults.* Deborah Tannen. Ballantine Books, 2002.

Getting Past No: Negotiating Your Way from Confrontation to Cooperation.
William Ury. Bantam Books, 1991.

How Families Work Together. Family Business Leadership Series, No. 4.
Mary F. Whiteside. Georgia: Business Owner Resources, 1993. To order,
call 800/551-0633.

*The Eight Essential Steps to Conflict Resolution: Preserving Relationships at
Work, at Home and in the Community.* Dudley Weeks. New York: G.P. Put-
nam's Sons, 1992.

Death

*What to Do When a Loved One Dies: A Practical and Compassionate Guide to
Dealing with Death on Life's Terms.* Eva Shaw. Dickens Press, 1994.

*Step by Step: Your Guide to Making Practical Decisions When a Loved One
Dies.* Ellen Shaw. Quality Life Resources, 2001.

Discretionary Grants

"Discretionary Grants," *Family Matters,* Summer 1998. Council on Foundations. To order, call 202/467-0407. Members can access online at
www.cof.org.

"Discretionary Grants: Encouraging Participation…or Dividing Families?"
Jason Born. *Passages: Exploring Key Issues in Family Giving, vol. 3.2.* National
Center for Family Philanthropy, 2001. To order, visit www.ncfp.org.

Beyond Our Borders: A Guide to Making Grants Outside the U.S. John Edie.
Council on Foundations, 2002. To order, call 888/239-5221 or visit
www.cof.org.

Family Foundations and the Law: What You Need to Know. John Edie. Council
on Foundations, 2002. To order, call 888/239-5221 or visit www.cof.org.

Donor Intent

Donor Intent: Interpreting the Founder's Vision. The Philanthropy Roundtable, 1993. To order, call 202/822-8333.

The Family Foundation Library series. Council on Foundations, 1997.
To order, call 888/239-5221, order #814 or visit www.cof.org.

*Living the Legacy: The Values of a Family's Philanthropy Across Generations.
National Center Journal, Volume 3.* National Center for Family Philanthropy, 2001. To order, call 202/293-3424 or visit www.ncfp.org.

Splendid Legacy: The Guide To Creating Your Family Foundation. National Center for Family Philanthropy, 2002. To order, call 202/293-3424 or visit www.ncfp.org.

Family Businesses

Developing Family Business Policies: Your Guide to the Future. Craig E.Aronoff, Joseph H. Astrachan and John L. Ward. Georgia: Business Owner Resources, 1998. To order, visit www.amazon.com

Keep the Family Baggage Out of the Family Business: Avoiding the Seven Deadly Sins That Destroy Family Businesses. Quentin Fleming. Simon & Schuster, 2000. To order, visit www.amazon.com.

Generation to Generation: Life Cycles of the Family Business. Kelin E. Gersick, Editor, John A. Davis and Marion McCollum Hampton. Harvard Business School Press, 1997.

Keeping the Family Business Healthy: How to Plan for Continuing Growth, Profitability and Family Leadership. John L. Ward. Jossey-Bass Management Series 1987. To order, visit www.amazon.com.

Legal

"Choreographing a Foundation Disappearing Act." Jane Nober. *Foundation News & Commentary*, May/June 2003. www.foundationnews.org.

"Conflicts of Interest." Jane Nober. *Foundation News & Commentary*, July/August 2003. www.foundationnews.org.

Family Foundations and the Law: What You Need to Know. Council on Foundations, 2002. To order, call 888/239-5221, order #805 or visit www.cof.org.

"Merging Ahead." Jane Nober. *Foundation News & Commentary*, January/February 2003. www.foundationnews.org.

Mission

"Communicating Missions and Guidelines to the Public," *Family Matters,* Spring 1999. Council on Foundations. Members can access online at www.cof.org.

The Family Advisor: Values, Vision and Mission. Council on Foundations, 2000. To order, call 202/467-0407 or e-mail family@cof.org.

Governance, Management, Grantmaking and Family Issues: Family Foundation Library series. Council on Foundations, 1997. To order, call 888/239-5221, order #814 or visit www.cof.org.

Voyage of Discovery: A Planning Workbook for Philanthropic Families. Judith Healy. National Center for Family Philanthropy, 2001. To order, call 202/293-3424 or visit www.ncfp.org.

Self-Assessment

The Drucker Foundation Self-Assessment Tool: Process Guide and Workbook. Gary J. Stern. Drucker Foundation and Jossey-Bass, Inc., 1999. To order, call 800/956-7739 or visit www.amazon.com.

Measuring Board Effectiveness. BoardSource (formerly National Center for Nonprofit Boards), 2000. To order, call 800/833-6262 or visit www.boardsource.org.

Self-Assessment for Foundation Boards. BoardSource, 2000. To order, call 800/883-6262 or visit www.boardsource.org.

Self-Study Guide for Family Foundation Boards. Council on Foundations, 1994. To order, call 888/239-5221, order #807 or visit www.cof.org.

Storytelling

"Sharing Our Stories." *Family Matters*, Fall 2002. Council on Foundations. Members can access online at www.cof.org.

The Family Advisor: Archiving Your Family History. Council on Foundations. To order a copy, call 202/467-0407 or e-mail family@cof.org.

Family Tales, Family Wisdom: How to Gather the Stories of a Lifetime and Share Them With Your Family. Robert Akeret. New York, NY: William Morrow and Company, 1991.

Donor Intent: Interpreting the Founder's Vision. The Philanthropy Roundtable, 1993. To order, call 202/822-8333.

Keeping Family Stories Alive: A Creative Guide to Taping Your Family Life & Lore. Vera Rosenbluth. Vancouver, BC: Hartley and Marks Publishers, 1990.

"Living the Legacy: The Values of a Family's Philanthropy Across Generations." *National Center Journal, Volume 3*. National Center for Family Philanthropy, 2001. To order, call 202/293-3424 or visit www.ncfp.org.

The Power of Personal Storytelling: Spinning Tales to Connect with Others. Jack Maguire. New York, NY: Jeremy Tarcher/Putnam, 1998.

Telling Your Own Stories: For Family and Classroom Storytelling, Public Speaking, and Personal Journaling. Donald Davis. Little Rock, AR: August House, 1993.

Succession

The Succession Workbook: Continuity Planning for Family Foundations. Council on Foundations, 2000. To order, call 888/239-5221, order #821 or visit www.cof.org.

The Giving Family: Raising Our Children to Help Others. Council on Foundations, 2001. To order, call 888/239-5221, order #822, or visit www.cof.org.

Family Foundations Now—And Forever? The Question of Intergenerational Succession. Council on Foundations, 1997. To order, call 888/239-5221, order #809, or visit www.cof.org.

The Family Advisor: Generational Succession. Council on Foundations. To order, call 202/467-0407 or e-mail family@cof.org.

Terminating and Splitting

"Rebuilding on a Firm Foundation," Betty Marton. *NYRAG Times*, Winter 1998/99. To order, visit www.nyrag.org.

"End of the Road? Alternatives to Perpetuity." *Family Matters*, Fall 1999. Council on Foundations. Members can access online at www.cof.org.

Should Foundations Live Forever?: The Question of Perpetuity. Martin Morse Wooster. Capital Research Center, 1998. To order, call 202/483-6900.

Ways Your Family Foundation Can Grow and Thrive. The Family Foundation Series. Council of Michigan Foundations, 1997. To order, visit www.cmif.org.

Closing a Foundation: The Lucille P. Markey Charitable Trust. John H. Dickason and Duncan Neuhauser, Council on Foundations, 2000. To order, call 888/239-5221 or visit www.cof.org.

Values and Vision

Ethical Choices for Family Foundations. Institute for Global Ethics, 2001. To order, call 888/239-5221, order #824 or visit www.cof.org.

The Family Advisor: Values and Ethics in Philanthropy. Council on Foundations, 2000. To order, call 202/467-0407 or e-mail family@cof.org.

Responsible Family Philanthropy: A Resource Book on Ethical Decisionmaking for Family Foundations. Michael Rion. Council on Foundations, 1998. To order, call 888/239-5221, order #854 or visit www.cof.org.

Small Foundation Management: From Groundwork to Grantmaking. Elaine Gast. Council on Foundations, 2002. To order, call 888/239-5221, order #826 or visit www.cof.org.

Network with Your Peers

There is an entire network of philanthropic organizations that can help foundations learn from one another—national organizations such as the Council on Foundations and the National Center for Family Philanthropy; geographically centered associations such as regional associations of grantmakers; affinity groups such as the Association of Small Foundations; and local organizations such as community foundations.

Council on Foundations

1828 L Street, NW, Suite #300
Washington, DC 20036
202/466-6512
www.cof.org

The national membership association for foundations and corporate giving programs, serving the public good by promoting and enhancing responsible and effective philanthropy. The Council provides the field with educational programs and publications, research, legal assistance, breaking news and personalized assistance.

Affinity Groups

Affinity groups and grantmaker associations represent a variety of different issues and population groups. They are sources of up-to-date grantmaking information in their areas of interest. Some groups emphasize networking and information exchange among members, while others advocate for an issue or cause. Generally, these groups serve grantmakers, although some include grantee organizations as members. The typical group is a network managed by volunteers, although a growing number are becoming non-profit organizations in their own right. For more information on affinity groups, contact the Council on Foundations' Affinity Group Services at 202/467-0398 or visit www.cof.org/index.cfm?containerid=72.

Association of Small Foundations

4905 Delray Avenue, Suite #308
Bethesda, MD 20814
301/907-3337 or 888/212-9922
www.smallfoundations.org

This membership organization provides information, assistance and workshops to foundations with few or no staff.

Forum of Regional Associations of Grantmakers

1111 19th Street, NW, Suite #650
Washington, DC 20036
202/467-1120
www.givingforum.org

A membership association of the nation's largest regional grantmaker associations, the Forum promotes expanded, effective philanthropy by enhancing the capacity of regional associations of grantmakers.

The Foundation Center

79 Fifth Avenue
New York, NY 10003-3076
212/620-4230
www.fdncenter.org

> *Field Offices*
> San Francisco: 415/397-0903
> Washington DC: 202/331-1400
> Atlanta: 404/880-0094
> Cleveland: 216/861-1933

The Foundation Center is an essential resource for grantseekers looking for information on appropriate funding sources for their programs and organizations. It focuses on furthering the public understanding of foundations by conducting research in the field.

Independent Sector

1200 18th Street, NW, Suite #200
Washington, DC 20036
202/467-6100
www.independentsector.org

Independent Sector is a nonprofit coalition of more than 850 corporate, foundation and voluntary organizations. Its mission is to create a national forum to encourage giving and volunteering by individuals and organizations.

Indiana University Center on Philanthropy
550 West North Street, Suite #301
Indianapolis, IN 46202-3162
317/274-4200
www.philanthropy.iupui.edu

This academic center is dedicated to increasing the understanding of philanthropy and improving its practice through research, teaching and public service.

National Center for Family Philanthropy
1220 19th Street, NW, Suite #300
Washington, DC 20036
202/293-3424
www.ncfp.org

This national organization provides research, educational materials and programs for families and individuals engaged in philanthropy.

National Network of Grantmakers
1717 Kettner Blvd. #110
San Diego, CA 92101
619/231-1348
www.nng.org

National Network of Grantmakers (NNG) is an organization of individuals involved in funding social and economic justice, not a funding group. NNG is committed to the goal of increasing resources—financial and otherwise—to organizations working for social change.

BoardSource (formerly National Center for Nonprofit Boards)
1828 L Street, NW, Suite #900
Washington, DC 20036
800/883-6262
www.boardsource.org

This association focuses on strengthening the effectiveness of nonprofit governing boards by providing information, resources and consulting services.

The Philanthropy Roundtable

1150 17th Street, NW, Suite #503
Washington, DC 20036
202/822-8333
www.philanthropyroundtable.org

This national association is founded on the principle that voluntary private action offers the best means of addressing society's needs, and that a vibrant private sector is critical to creating the wealth that makes philanthropy possible.

Worldwide Initiatives for Grantmaker Support (WINGS)

c/o European Foundation Centre
51 rue de la Concorde
Brussels B-1050 Belgium
32/2-512-8938
www.wingsweb.org

Worldwide Initiatives for Grantmaker Support (WINGS) is a global network of more than 100 membership associations serving grantmakers and support organizations serving philanthropy.

Turn to the Council on Foundations

As your foundation evolves, it will be faced with many questions: What are our giving options? Who should be included on the board? How should the foundation be managed?

With more than 50 years of service, the Council on Foundations can help evolving foundations find answers to these questions. The Council's services support donors, family members, trustees, staff and colleagues—anyone working to strengthen foundation work.

Become more efficient and effective with the Council's individualized assistance, professional development, peer-networking opportunities, publications and our premier annual events.

What the Council Can Do for You

Individualized Assistance

Get timely and personalized answers to your questions about governance, management, grantmaking, legal issues, succession, family dynamics and more. Our clearinghouse of information, including an extensive collection of articles, sample policies, grants guidelines, position descriptions and other resources, can serve as your own foundation's library.

Professional Development

The Council offers you a variety of educational opportunities for veteran and beginning staff and board members, including the following annual and semiannual programs:

- Family Foundation Conference, the only national gathering for family foundations
- Next Generation Retreat, a must-attend event for new and soon-to-be family board members
- Institute for New Grantmakers, a jump-start for new grantmakers or those with less than three years of experience
- Institute for New Board Members, an orientation for new trustees
- Community Foundation Conference, the premier national event for community foundations, most of which can establish donor-advised funds.
- Center for Community Foundation Excellence (CCFE) Courses

- State-of-the-art training in the following areas:
  - Foundation basics
  - Generational succession
  - Board responsibilities
  - Legal issues for foundations
  - Trends in family foundations
  - Working with the media
  - Family foundations and ethics
  - Instilling philanthropic values in children
  - Management options
  - Research
  - Grantmaking process (from application to evaluation and every step in between).

Peer Networking and Leadership Opportunities

Learn from your peers by participating in our committees, conferences and e-mail lists—broaden your connection and exchange practical tips. You can also share your expertise as a speaker, moderator, facilitator or session designer at one of our conferences.

Professional Resources

The Council is your primary source for critical literature in the field:

- *Family Matters*, a quarterly newsletter that explores topics facing family foundations and offers a vehicle for the field to share experiences
- *The Family Advisor*, a series of information packets that address issues such as grant evaluations, mission statements, and investment policies
- *Hot Topics*, a periodic electronic newsletter designed to keep you abreast of the latest issues affecting family foundations
- *Board Briefings*, a quarterly issue paper that gives your board a user-friendly resource to prompt discussion and take a stance
- *Washington Update*, an e-newsletter that keeps you aware of legislative issues and initiatives affecting the philanthropic world